"Have you ever read the Christian Bible?"

"No, read it to me," said Gasan.

The student opened the Bible and read from St. Matthew: "And why take ye thought for raiment? Consider the lilies of the field, how they grow. They toil not, neither do they spin, and yet I say unto you that even Solomon in all his glory was not arrayed like one of these. . . ."

Gasan said: "Whoever uttered those words, I consider an enlightened man."

The GOSPEL *According to* ZEN

beyond the death of god

ROBERT SOHL · AUDREY CARR

EDITORS

A MENTOR BOOK from
NEW AMERICAN LIBRARY
TIMES MIRROR
New York and Toronto
The New English Library Limited, London

ACKNOWLEDGMENTS

"The Most Serious Question of All" and "The Sound of
One Hand" from *Zen Flesh, Zen Bones* by Paul Reps.
Reprinted by permission of Charles E. Tuttle Co., Inc.

"Today's Spiritual Crisis," "A Religious Man," "An Artist
of Life," and "East and West" from pp. 1-5, 11-12, 15-16,
78-80, 92 in *Zen Buddhism and Psychoanalysis* by Erich
Fromm, D. T. Suzuki and Richard de Martino. Copyright © 1960 by Erich Fromm. Reprinted by permission
of Harper & Row, Publishers, and George Allen & Unwin
Ltd.

"What is Zen?" and "Satori" from *An Introduction to Zen
Buddhism* by D. T. Suzuki. Reprinted by permission of
Grove Press, Inc. and Hutchinson Publishing Group Ltd.
All rights reserved.

"Wash Out Your Mouth," "Beyond Theology," and "This
Is My Body" from *Beyond Theology* by Alan Watts.
© Copyright 1964 by Alan Watts. Reprinted by permis-
sion of Pantheon Books, a Division of Random House,
Inc., and Hodder & Stoughton, Ltd.

"The Zenrin" and "Instant Zen" from *Haiku*, vol. I. ed.
R. H. Blyth. Reprinted by permission of The Hokuseido
Press.

"The Chess Game" from *A First Zen Reader* by Trevor
Leggett. Reprinted by permission of Charles E. Tuttle
Co., Inc.

"Salvation or Satori" from *The Supreme Doctrine* by
Hubert Benoit. © Copyright 1955 by Pantheon Books,

*(The following pages constitute a continuation
of this copyright page.)*

MENTOR TRADEMARK REG. U.S. PAT. OFF. AND FOREIGN COUNTRIES
REGISTERED TRADEMARK—MARCA REGISTRADA
HECHO EN CHICAGO, U.S.A.

SIGNET, SIGNET CLASSIC, MENTOR AND PLUME BOOKS
are published
in the United States by The New American Library, Inc.,
1301 Avenue of the Americas, New York, New York 10019.,
in Canada by The New American Library
of Canada Limited,
295 King Street East, Toronto 2, Ontario,
in the United Kingdom by The New English
Library Limited,
Barnard's Inn, Holborn, London, E.C. 1, England

First Printing, April, 1970

PRINTED IN THE UNITED STATES OF AMERICA

IN MEMORY OF

D. T. Suzuki and R. H. Blyth

CONTENTS

4

5

6

The Most Serious Question of All

The Most Serious
Question of All

PROVIDED he makes and wins an argument about Buddhism with those who live there, any wandering monk can remain in a Zen temple. If he is defeated, he has to move on.

In a temple in the northern part of Japan two brother monks were dwelling together. The elder one was learned, but the younger one was stupid and had but one eye.

A wandering monk came and asked for lodging, properly challenging them to a debate about the sublime teaching. The elder brother, tired that day from much studying, told the younger one to take his place. "Go and request the dialogue in silence," he cautioned.

So the young monk and the stranger went to the shrine and sat down.

Shortly afterward the traveler rose and went in to the elder brother and said: "Your young brother is a wonderful fellow. He defeated me."

"Relate the dialogue to me," said the elder one.

"Well," explained the traveler, "first I held up one finger, representing Buddha, the enlightened one. So he held up two fingers, signifying Buddha and his teaching. I held up three fingers, representing Buddha, his teaching, and his followers, living the harmonious life. Then he shook his clenched fist in my face, indicating that all three come from one realization. Thus he won and so I have no right to remain here." With this, the traveler left.

"Where is that fellow?" asked the younger one, running in to his elder brother.

"I understand you won the debate."

"Won nothing. I'm going to beat him up."

"Tell me the subject of the debate," asked the elder one.

"Why, the minute he saw me he held up one finger, insulting me by insinuating that I have only one eye. Since he was a stranger I thought I would be polite to him, so I held up two fingers, congratulating him that he has two eyes. Then the impolite wretch held up three fingers, suggesting that between us we only have three eyes. So I got mad and started to punch him, but he ran out and that ended it!"

Mumon's comment: The stranger is like the wise theologian who preaches the death of God. Although his words are most eloquent his degree of attainment is obvious. The one-eyed brother is like the pious churchman who worships God and asks him to solve his problems. His motives are pure but his one eye is a handicap. Now suppose you were to decide the winner of this debate. If your decision is correct the death of God will be a joke too funny to laugh at. On the other hand, if you cannot choose between the two no God will be powerful enough to save you from your fate.

> *Is God dead or not?*
> *This is the most serious question of all.*
> *If you say yes or no,*
> *You lose your own Buddha-nature.*

1

Today's Spiritual Crisis

WHILE THE MAJORITY of people living in the West do not consciously feel as if they were living through a crisis of Western culture (probably never have the majority of people in a radically critical situation been aware of the crisis), there is agreement, at least among a number of critical observers, as to the existence and the nature of this crisis. It is the crisis which has been described as *malaise, ennui, mal du siecle,* the deadening of life, the automatization of man, his alienation from himself, from his fellowman and from nature. Man has followed rationalism to the point where rationalism has transformed itself into utter irrationality. Since Descartes, man has increasingly split thought from affect; thought alone is considered rational—affect, by its very nature, irrational; the person, *I*, has been split off into an intellect, which constitutes my self, and which is to control *me* as it is to control nature. Control by the intellect over nature, and the production of more and more things, became the paramount aims of life. In the process man has transformed himself into a thing, life has become subordinated to property, "to be" is dominated by "to have." Where the roots of Western culture, both Greek and Hebrew, considered the aim of life the *perfection of man,* modern man is concerned with the *perfection of things,* and the knowledge of how to make them. Western man is in a state of schizoid inability to experience affect, hence he is anxious, depressed, and desperate. He still pays lip service to the aims of happiness, individualism, initiative—but actually he has no aim. Ask him what he is living for, what is the aim of all his strivings—and he will be embarrassed. Some may say they live for the family, others, "to have fun," still others, to make money, but in reality nobody knows what he is living for; he has no goal, except the wish to escape insecurity and aloneness.

It is true, church membership today is higher than ever before, books on religion become best sellers, and more people speak of God than ever before. Yet this kind of religious profession only covers up a profoundly materialistic and irreligious attitude, and is to be understood as an ideological reaction—caused by insecurity and conformism—to the trend of the nineteenth century, which Nietzsche characterized by his famous "God is dead." As a truly religious attitude, it has no reality.

The abandonment of theistic ideas in the nineteenth century was—seen from one angle—no small achievement. Man took a big plunge into objectivity. The earth ceased to be the center of the universe; man lost his central role of the creature destined by God to dominate all other creatures. Studying man's hidden motivations with a new objectivity, Freud recognized that the faith in an all-powerful, omniscient God had its root in the helplessness of human existence and in man's attempt to cope with his helplessness by means of belief in a helping father and mother represented by God in heaven. He saw that man only can save himself; the teaching of the great teachers, the loving help of parents, friends, and loved ones can help him—but can help him only to dare to accept the challenge of existence and to react to it with all his might and all his heart.

Man gave up the illusion of a fatherly God as a parental helper—but he gave up also the true aims of all great humanistic religions: overcoming the limitations of an egotistical self, achieving love, objectivity, and humility and respecting life so that the aim of life is living itself, and man becomes what he potentially is. These were the aims of the great Western religions, as they were the aims of the great Eastern religions. The East, however, was not burdened with the concept of a transcendent father-savior in which the monotheistic religions expressed their longings. Taoism and Buddhism had a rationality and realism superior to that of the Western religions. They could see man realistically and objectively, having nobody but the "awakened" ones to guide him, and being able to be guided because each man has within himself the capacity to awake and be enlightened. This is precisely the reason why Eastern religious thought, Taoism and Buddhism—and their blending in Zen Buddhism—assume such importance for the West today. Zen Buddhism helps man to find an answer to the question of his existence, an answer which is essentially the same as that given in the Judeo-Christian tradition, and yet which does not contradict the rationality, realism, and independence which are modern man's precious achievements. Paradoxically, Eastern religious thought turns out to be more congenial to Western rational thought than does Western religious thought itself.

—Erich Fromm

What Is Zen?

Is ZEN a system of philosophy, highly intellectual and profoundly metaphysical, as most Buddhist teachings are?

I have already stated that we find in Zen all the philosophy of the East crystallized, but this ought not to be taken as meaning that Zen is a philosophy in the ordinary application of the term. Zen is decidedly not a system founded upon logic and analysis. If anything, it is the antipode to logic, by which I mean the dualistic mode of thinking. There may be an intellectual element in Zen, for Zen is the whole mind, and in it we find a great many things; but the mind is not a composite thing that is to be divided into so many faculties, leaving nothing behind when the dissection is over. Zen has nothing to teach us in the way of intellectual analysis; nor has it any set doctrines which are imposed on its followers for acceptance. In this respect Zen is quite chaotic if you choose to say so. Probably Zen followers may have sets of doctrines, but they have them on their own account, and for their own benefit; they do not owe the fact to Zen. Therefore, there are in Zen no sacred books or dogmatic tenets, nor are there any symbolic formulae through which an access might be gained into the signification of Zen. If I am asked, then, what Zen teaches, I would answer, Zen teaches nothing. Whatever teachings there are in Zen, they come out of one's own mind. We teach ourselves; Zen merely points the way. Unless this pointing is teaching, there is certainly nothing in Zen purposely set up as its cardinal doctrines or as its fundamental philosophy.

Zen claims to be Buddhism, but all the Buddhist teachings as propounded in the sutras and sastras are treated by Zen as mere waste paper whose utility consists in wiping off the dirt of intellect and nothing more. Do not imagine, however, that Zen is nihilism. All nihilism is self-destructive, it ends nowhere. Negativism is sound as method, but the highest truth is an affirmation. When it is said that Zen has no philosophy, that it denies all doctrinal authority, that it casts aside all so-called sacred literature as rubbish, we must not forget that Zen is holding up in this very act of negation something quite positive and eternally affirmative. This will become clearer as we proceed.

Is Zen a religion? It is not a religion in the sense that the term is popularly understood; for Zen has no God to worship, no ceremonial rites to observe, no future abode to which the dead are destined, and, last of all, Zen has no soul whose welfare is to be looked after by somebody else and whose immortality is a matter of intense concern with some people. Zen is free from all these dogmatic and "religious" encumbrances.

When I say there is no God in Zen, the pious reader may be shocked, but this does not mean that Zen denies the existence of God; neither denial nor affirmation concerns Zen. When a thing is denied, the very denial involves something not denied. The same can be said of affirmation. This is inevitable in logic. Zen wants to rise above logic, Zen wants to find a higher affirmation where there are no antitheses. Therefore, in Zen, God is neither denied nor insisted upon; only there is in Zen no such God as has been conceived by Jewish and Christian minds. For the same reason that Zen is not a philosophy, Zen is not a religion.

As to all those images of various Buddhas and Bodhisattvas and Devas and other beings that one comes across in Zen temples, they are like so many pieces of wood or stone or metal; they are like the camellias, azaleas, or stone lanterns in my garden. Make obeisance to the camellia now in full bloom, and worship it if you like, Zen would say. There is as much religion in so doing as in bowing to the various Buddhist gods, or as in sprinkling holy water, or as in participating in the Lord's Supper. All those pious deeds considered to be meritorious or sanctifying by most so-called religiously minded people are artificialities in the eyes of Zen. It boldly declares that "the immaculate Yogins do not enter Nirvana and the precept-violating monks do not go to hell." This, to ordinary minds, is a contradiction of the common law of moral life, but herein lies the truth and life of Zen. Zen is the spirit of a man. Zen believes in his inner purity and goodness. Whatever is superadded or violently torn away, injures the wholesomeness of the spirit. Zen, therefore, is emphatically against all religious conventionalism.

—D. T. Suzuki

Wash Out Your Mouth

CHRISTIAN PIETY makes a strange image of the object of its devotion, "Jesus Christ, and Him crucified." Him. The bearded moralist with the stern, kind, and vaguely hurt look in the eyes. The man with the lantern, knocking at the heart's door. "Come along now, boys! Enough of this horsing around! It's time you and I had a very serious talk." Christ Jesus our Lord. *Jeez*-us. Jeez-*you*. The Zen Buddhists say, "Wash out your mouth every time you say 'Buddha!'" The new life for Christianity begins just as soon as someone can get up in church and say, "Wash out your mouth every time you say 'Jesus!'"

For we are spiritually paralyzed by the fetish of Jesus. Even to atheists he is the supremely good man, the exemplar and moral authority with whom no one may disagree. Whatever our opinions, we must perforce wangle the words of Jesus to agree with them. Poor Jesus! If he had known how great an authority was to be projected upon him, he would never have said a word. His literary image in the Gospels has, through centuries of homage, become far more of an idol than anything graven in wood or stone, so that today the most genuinely reverent act of worship is to destroy that image. In his own words, "It is expedient for you that I go away, for if I go not away, the Paraclete [the Holy Spirit] cannot come unto you." Or, as the angel said to the disciples who came looking for the body of Jesus in the tomb, "Why do you seek the living among the dead? He is not here. He is risen and has gone before you. . . ." But Christian piety does not let him go away, and continues to seek the living Christ in the dead letter of the historical record. As he said to the Jews, "You search the scriptures, for in them you *think* you have eternal life."

The Crucifixion gives eternal life because it is the giving up of God as an object to be possessed, known, and held to for one's own safety, "for he that would save his soul shall lose it." To cling to Jesus is therefore to worship a Christ uncrucified, an idol instead of the living God.

—Alan Watts

A Religious Man

I HAVE SAID that man is asked a question by the very fact of his existence, and that this is a question raised by the contradiction within himself—that of being in nature and at the same time of transcending nature by the fact that he is life aware of itself. Any man who listens to this question posed to him, and who makes it a matter of "ultimate concern" to answer this question, and to answer it as a whole man and not only by thoughts, is a "religious" man; and all systems that try to give, teach, and transmit such answers are "religions." On the other hand, any man—and any culture—that tries to be deaf to the existential question is irreligious. There is no better example that can be cited for men who are deaf to the question posed by existence than we ourselves, living in the twentieth century. We try to evade the question by concern with property, prestige, power, production, fun, and, ultimately, by trying to forget that we—that I—exist. No matter how often he *thinks* of God or goes to church, or how much he believes in religious ideas, if he, the whole man, is deaf to the question of existence, if he does not have an answer to it, he is marking time, and he lives and dies like one of the million things he produces. He *thinks* of God, instead of experiencing *being* God.

—Erich Fromm

An Artist of Life

WE CANNOT ALL be expected to be scientists, but
we are so constituted by nature that we can all be
artists—not, indeed, artists of special kinds, such as
painters, sculptors, musicians, poets, etc., but artists
of life. This profession, "artist of life," may sound
new and quite odd, but in point of fact we are all
born artists of life and, not knowing it, most of us
fail to be so and the result is that we make a mess
of our lives, asking, "What is the meaning of life?"
"Are we not facing blank nothingness?" "After living seventy-eight, or even ninety, years, where do
we go? Nobody knows," etc., etc. I am told that most
modern men and women are neurotic on this account. But the Zen-man can tell them that they all
have forgotten that they are born artists, creative
artists of life, and that as soon as they realize this
fact and truth they will all be cured of neurosis or
psychosis or whatever name they have for their
trouble.

What then is meant by being an artist of life?

Artists of any kind, as far as we know, have to use
one instrument or another to express themselves, to
demonstrate their creativity in one form or another.
The sculptor has to have stone or wood or clay and
the chisel or some other tools to impress his ideas on
the material. But an artist of life has no need of

going out of himself. All the material, all the implements, all the technical skill that are ordinarily required are with him from the time of his birth, perhaps even before his parents gave him birth. This is unusual, extraordinary, you may exclaim. But when you think about this for a while you will, I am sure, realize what I mean. If you do not, I will be more explicit and tell you this: the body, the physical body we all have, is the material, corresponding to the painter's canvas, the sculptor's wood or stone or clay, the musician's violin or flute, the singer's vocal cords. And everything that is attached to the body, such as the hands, the feet, the trunk of the body, the head, the viscera, the nerves, the cells, thoughts, feelings, senses—everything, indeed, that goes to make up the whole personality—is both the material on which and the instruments with which the person molds his creative genius into conduct, into behavior, into all forms of action, indeed into life itself. To such a person his life reflects every image he creates out of his inexhaustive source of the unconscious. To such, his every deed expresses originality, creativity, his living personality. There is in it no conventionality, no conformity, no inhibitory motivation. He moves just as he pleases. His behavior is like the wind which bloweth as it listeth. He has no self encased in his fragmentary, limited, restrained, egocentric existence. He is gone out of this prison. One of the great Zen masters of the T'ang says: "With a man who is master of himself wherever he may be found he behaves truly to himself." This man I call the true artist of life.

His Self has touched the unconscious, the source

of infinite possibilities. His is "no-mind." Says St. Augustine, "Love God and do what you will." This corresponds to the poem of Bunan, the Zen master of the seventeenth century:

> While alive
> Be a dead man,
> Thoroughly dead;
> And act as you will,
> And all is good.

To love God is to have no self, to be of no-mind, to become "a dead man," to be free from the constrictive motivations of consciousness. This man's "Good morning" has no human element of any kind of vested interest. He is addressed and he responds. He feels hungry and eats. Superficially, he is a natural man, coming right out of nature with no complicated ideologies of modern civilized man. But how rich his inward life is! Because it is in direct communion with the great unconscious.

—D. T. Suzuki

Beyond Theology

WHEN GOD IS DEAD, man, who was always defined as a creature other than God, begins to feel himself as other than reality—a sentimental irregularity in a dog-eat-dog system that might have been contrived by the Devil, if Devil there were. Men so at odds with their environment must either bulldoze it into obedience or destroy it. The two choices come to the same thing.

But a superior religion goes beyond theology. It turns toward the center; it investigates and feels out the inmost depths of man himself, since it is here that we are in most intimate contact, or rather, in *identity* with existence itself. Dependence on theological ideas and symbols is replaced by direct, nonconceptual *touch* with a level of being which is simultaneously one's own and the being of all others. For at the point where I am most myself I am most beyond myself. At root I am one with all the other branches. Yet this level of being is not something to be grasped and categorized, to be inspected, analyzed or made an object of knowledge—not because it is taboo or sacrosanct, but because it is the point *from* which one radiates, the light not before but within the eyes. . . .

There is, then, a more structural and objective

foundation for that leap of faith in which a man may dare to think that he is not a stranger in the universe, nor a solitary and tragic flash of awareness in endless and overwhelming darkness. For in the light of what we now know in physical terms, it is not unreasonable to wager that deep down at the center "I myself" is "It"—as in "as *it* was in the beginning, is now and ever shall be, world without end."

If this is a hope, or a fervent belief, Krishnamurti is right in saying that it should be challenged and tested with the question, "Why do you want to believe that? Is it because you are afraid of dying, of coming to an end? Is this identification with the cosmic Self the last desperate resort of your ego to continue its game?" Indeed, if this Supreme Identity is, for me, a belief to which I am clinging, I am in total self-contradiction. Not only is there no sense in clinging to what I am; the very act of clinging also implies that I do not really know that I *am* it! Such belief is merely doubt dressed up. The final meaning of negative theology, of knowing God by unknowing, of the abandonment of idols both sensible and conceptual, is that ultimate faith is not in or upon anything at all. It is complete letting go. Not only is it beyond theology; it is also beyond atheism and nihilism. Such letting go cannot be attained. It cannot be acquired or developed through perseverance and exercises, except insofar as such efforts prove the impossibility of acquiring it. Letting go comes only through desperation. When you know that it is beyond you—beyond your powers of action as beyond your powers of relaxation. When you give

23

up every last trick and device for getting it, including this "giving up" as something that one might *do*, say, at ten o'clock tonight. That you cannot by any means do it—that is it! *That* is the mighty self-abandonment which gives birth to the stars.

—Alan Watts

2

The Zenrin

Nothing whatever is hidden;
  From of old, all is clear as daylight.

The old pine-tree speaks divine wisdom;
  The secret bird manifests eternal truth.

There is no place to seek the mind;
  It is like the footprints of the birds in the sky.

Above, not a piece of tile to cover the head;
  Beneath, not an inch of earth to put one's foot on.

Sitting quietly, doing nothing,
  Spring comes, and the grass grows by itself.

The water before, and the water after,
  Now and forever flowing, follow each other.

One word determines the whole world;
  One sword pacifies heaven and earth.

If you do not get it from yourself,
   Where will you go for it?

If you wish to know the road up the mountain,
   You must ask the man who goes back and forth
      on it.

Falling mist flies together with the wild ducks;
   The waters of autumn are of one color with the
      sky.

If you don't believe, just look at September, look at
      October!
   The yellow leaves falling, falling, to fill both
      mountain and river.

The wild geese do not intend to cast their reflection;
   The water has no mind to receive their image.

Scoop up the water and the moon is in your hands;
   Hold the flowers and your clothes are scented with
      them.

Mountains and rivers, the whole earth,—
   All manifest forth the essence of being.

The voice of the mountain torrent is from one great
    tongue;
  The lines of the hills, are they not the Pure Body
    of Buddha?

In the vast inane there is no back or front;
  The path of the bird annihilates East and West.

From of old there were not two paths;
  "Those who have arrived" all walked the same
    road.

Day after day the sun rises in the east;
  Day after day it sets in the west.

Ever onwards to where the waters have an end;
  Waiting motionless for when the white clouds
    shall arise.

Wind subsiding, the flowers still fall;
  Bird crying, the mountain silence deepens.

To save life it must be destroyed.
  When utterly destroyed, one dwells for the first
    time in peace.

Taking up one blade of grass,
  Use it as a sixteen-foot golden Buddha.

Heat does not wait for the sun, to be hot.
  Nor wind the moon, to be cool.

If you do not kill him,
  You will be killed by him.

To be conscious of the original mind, the original
      nature—
  Just this is the great disease of Zen!

Like a sword that cuts, but cannot cut itself;
  Like an eye that sees, but cannot see itself.

Perceiving the sun in the midst of the rain;
  Ladling out clear water from the depths of the
      fire.

Ride your horse along the edge of a sword;
  Hide yourself in the middle of the flames.

You cannot get it by taking thought;
  You cannot seek it by not taking thought.

It is like a tiger, but with many horns;
　　Like a cow, but it has no tail.

Draw water, and you think the mountains are
　　moving;
　　Raise the sail, and you think the cliffs are on the
　　run.

The blue hills are of themselves blue hills;
　　The white clouds are of themselves white clouds.

In the landscape of spring there is neither high nor
　　low;
　　The flowering branches grow naturally, some
　　long, some short.

Alive, I will not receive the Heavenly Halls;
　　Dead, I fear no Hell.

He holds the handle of the hoe, but his hands are
　　empty;
　　He rides astride the water-buffalo, but he is
　　walking.

Entering the forest he moves not the grass;
　　Entering the water he makes not a ripple.

31

If you meet an enlightened man in the street,
  Do not greet him with words, nor with silence.

Meeting, they laugh and laugh—
  The forest grove, the many fallen leaves!

We sleep with both legs outstretched,
  Free of the true, free of the false.

For long years a bird in a cage,
  Today, flying along with the clouds.

Satori

THE OBJECT of Zen discipline consists in acquiring a new viewpoint for looking into the essence of things. If you have been in the habit of thinking logically according to the rules of dualism, rid yourself of it and you may come around somewhat to the viewpoint of Zen. You and I are supposedly living in the same world, but who can tell that the thing we popularly call a stone that is lying before my window is the same to both of us? You and I sip a cup of tea. That act is apparently alike to us both, but who can tell what a wide gap there is subjectively between your drinking and my drinking? In your drinking there may be no Zen, while mine is brim-full of it. The reason for it is: you move in a logical circle and I am out of it. Though there is in fact nothing new in the so-called new viewpoint of Zen, the term "new" is convenient to express the Zen way of viewing the world, but its use here is a condescension on the part of Zen.

This acquiring of a new viewpoint in Zen is called *satori* (*wu* in Chinese) and its verb form is *satoru*. Without it there is no Zen, for the life of Zen begins with the "opening of *satori*." *Satori* may be defined as intuitive looking-into, in contradistinction to intellectual and logical understanding. Whatever the definition, *satori* means the unfolding of a new world hitherto unperceived in the confusion of a dualistic mind. With this preliminary remark I wish the reader to ponder the following *mondo* (literally, "asking and answering"), which I hope will illustrate my statement.

A young monk asked Joshu to be instructed in the faith of Zen. Said the master:

"Have you had your breakfast, or not?"

"Yes, master, I have," answered the monk.

"Go and get your bowls washed," was the immediate response. And this suggestion at once opened the monk's mind to the truth of Zen.

Later on Ummon commented on the response, saying: "Was there any special instruction in this remark by Joshu, or was there not? If there was, what was it? If there was not, what *satori* was it which the monk attained?" Still later Suigan had the following retort on Ummon: "The great master Ummon does not know what is what; hence this comment of his. It is altogether unnecessary; it is like painting legs to a snake, or painting a beard to the eunuch. My view differs from his. That monk who seems to have attained a sort of *satori* goes to hell as straight as an arrow!"

What does all this mean—Joshu's remark about washing the bowls, the monk's attainment of *satori,* Ummon's alternatives, and Suigan's assurance? Are they speaking against one another, or is it much ado about nothing? To my mind, they are all pointing one way and the monk may go anywhere, but his *satori* is not to no purpose.

Tokusan was a great scholar of the *Diamond Sutra.* Learning that there was such a thing as Zen, ignoring all the written scriptures and directly laying hands on one's soul, he went to Ryutan to be instructed in the teaching. One day Tokusan was sitting outside trying to look into the mystery of Zen. Ryutan said, "Why don't you come in?" Replied Tokusan, "It is pitch dark." A candle was lighted and held out to Tokusan. When he was at the point of taking it Ryutan suddenly blew out the light, whereupon the mind of Tokusan was opened.

Hyakujo (Pai-chang) went out one day attending his master Baso (Ma-tsu), when they saw a flock of wild geese flying. Baso asked:

"What are they?"

"They are wild geese, sir."

"Whither are they flying?"

"They have flown away."

Baso, abruptly taking hold of Hyakujo's nose, gave it a twist. Overcome with pain, Hyakujo cried out: "Oh! Oh!"

Said Baso, "You say they have flown away, but all the same they have been here from the very first."

This made Hyakujo's back wet with perspiration; he had *satori*.

Is there any possible connection between the washing of the bowls and the blowing out of the candle and the twisting of the nose? We must say with Ummon: If there is none, how could they have all come to a realization of the truth of Zen? If there is, what is the inner relationship? What is this *satori*? What new point of view of looking at things is this?

Under Daiye (Ta-hui), the great Zen master of the Sung dynasty, there was a monk named Doken

(Tao-ch'ien), who had spent many years in the study of Zen, but who had not as yet uncovered its secrets, if there were any. He was quite discouraged when he was sent on an errand to a distant city. A trip requiring half a year to finish would be a hindrance rather than a help to his study. Sogen (Tsung-yuan), one of his fellow students, was most sympathetic and said, "I will accompany you on this trip and do all I can for you; there is no reason why you cannot go on with your meditation even while traveling." One evening Doken despairingly implored his friend to assist him in the solution of the mystery of life. The friend said, "I am willing to help you in every way I can, but there are some things in which I cannot be of any help to you; these you must look after for yourself." Doken expressed the desire to know what these things were. Said his friend: "For instance, when you are hungry or thirsty, my eating of food or drinking will not fill your stomach; you must eat and drink for yourself. When you want to respond to the calls of nature you must take care of yourself, for I cannot be of any use to you. And then it will be nobody else but yourself that will carry your body along this highway." This friendly counsel at once opened the mind of the truth-seeking monk, who was so transported with his discovery that he did not know how to express his joy. Sogen said that his work was now done and that his further companionship would have no meaning after this; so he left Doken to continue his journey all by himself. After a half year Doken returned to his own monastery. Daiye, on his way down the mountains, happened to meet Doken and at once made the following remark, "This time he knows it all." What was it, let me ask, that flashed through Doken's mind when his friend Sogen gave him such matter-of-fact advice?

Kyogen (Hsiang-yen) was a disciple of Hyakujo (Pai-chang). After his master's death Kyogen went to Yisan (Kuei-shan), who had been a senior disciple of Hyakujo. Yisan asked him: "I am told that you have been studying under my late master, and also that you have remarkable intelligence. The understanding of Zen through this medium necessarily ends in intellectual analytical comprehension, which is not of much use; but nevertheless you may have had an insight into the truth of Zen. Let me have your view as to the reason of birth and death; that is, as to your own being before your parents had given birth to you."

Thus asked, Kyogen did not know how to reply. He retired into his own room and assiduously made research into the notes which he had taken of the sermons given by their late master. He failed to come across a suitable passage which he might present as his own view. He returned to Yisan and implored him to teach him in the faith of Zen, but Yisan replied: "I really have nothing to impart to you, and if I tried to do so you might have occasion to make me an object of ridicule. Besides, whatever I can tell you is my own and can never be yours." Kyogen was disappointed and considered him unkind. Finally he came to the decision to burn up all his notes and memoranda, which seemed to be of no help to his spiritual welfare, and, retiring altogether from the world, to spend the rest of his life in solitude and the simple life in accordance with Buddhist rules. He reasoned: "What is the use of studying Buddhism, which is so difficult to comprehend and which is too subtle to receive as instruction from another? I will be a plain homeless monk, troubled with no desire to master things too deep for thought." He left Yisan and built a hut near the tomb of Chu, the National Master at Nan-yang. One day he was seeding and sweeping the ground when a pebble which he had swept away struck a bamboo; the unexpected sound produced by the percussion elevated his mind to a state of *satori*. His joy was boundless. The question proposed by Yisan became transparent; he felt as if meeting his lost parents. Besides, he came to realize the kindness of Yisan in refusing him instruction, for now he realized that this experience could not have happened to him if Yisan had been unkind enough to explain things to him.

Cannot Zen be so explained that a master can lead all his pupils to enlightenment through explanation? Is *satori* something that is not at all capable of intellectual analysis? Yes, it is an experience which no amount of explanation or argument can make communicable to others unless the latter themselves had it previously. If *satori* is amenable to analysis in the sense that by so doing it becomes perfectly clear to another who has never had it, that *satori* will be no *satori*. For a *satori* turned into a concept ceases to be itself; and there will no more be a Zen experience. Therefore, all that we can do in Zen in the way of instruction is to indicate, or to suggest, or to show the way so that one's attention may be directed toward the goal. As to attaining the goal and taking hold of the thing itself, this must be done by one's own hands, for nobody else can do it for one. As regards the indication, it lies everywhere. When a man's mind is matured for *satori* it tumbles over one everywhere. An inarticulate sound, an unintelligent remark, a blooming flower, or a trivial incident such as stumbling is the condition or occasion that will open his mind to *satori*. Apparently, an insignificant event produces an effect which in importance is altogether out of proportion. The light touch of an igniting wire, and an explosion follows which will shake the very foundation of the earth. All the causes, all the conditions of *satori* are in the mind; they are merely waiting for the maturing. When the mind is ready for some reasons or others, a bird flies, or a bell rings, and you at once return to your original home; that is, you discover your now real self. From the very beginning nothing has been kept from you, all that you wished to see has been there all the time before you, it was only yourself that closed the eye to the fact. Therefore, there is in Zen nothing to explain, nothing to teach, that will add to your knowledge. Unless it grows out of yourself no knowledge is really yours, it is only a borrowed plumage.

Kozankoku (Huang Shan-ku), a Confucian poet and statesman of the Sung, came to Kwaido (Hui-t'ang) to be initiated into Zen. Said the Zen master: "There is a passage in the text with which you are perfectly familiar which fitly describes the teaching of Zen. Did not Confucius declare: 'Do you think I am hiding things from you, O my disciples? Indeed, I have nothing to hide from you.'" Kozankoku tried to answer, but Kwaido immediately checked him by saying, "No, no!" The Confucian scholar felt troubled in mind but did not know how to express himself. Some time later they were having a walk in the mountains; the wild laurel was in full bloom and the air was redolent with its scent. Asked the Zen master, "Do you smell it?" When the Confucian answered affirmatively, Kwaido said, "There, I have nothing to hide from you." This reminder at once led Kozankoku's mind to the opening of a *satori*.

These examples will suffice to show what *satori* is and how it unfolds itself. The reader may ask, however: "After the perusal of all your explanations or indications, we are not a whit wiser. Can you not definitely describe the content of *satori*, if there is any? Your examples and statements are tentative enough, but we simply know how the wind blows; where is the port the boat finally makes for?" To this the Zen devotee may answer: "As far as content goes, there is none in either *satori* or Zen that can be described or presented or demonstrated for your intellectual appreciation." For Zen has no business with ideas, and *satori* is a sort of inner perception— not the perception, indeed, of a single individual object but the perception of Reality itself, so to speak. The ultimate destination of *satori* is toward the Self; it has no other end but to be back within oneself. Therefore, said Joshu, "Have a cup of tea." Therefore, said Nansen, "This is such a good sickle, it cuts so well." This is the way the Self functions, and it must be caught, if at all catchable, in the midst of its functioning.

As *satori* strikes at the primary root of existence,

its attainment generally marks a turning point in one's life. The attainment, however, must be thoroughgoing and clear-cut; a lukewarm *satori*, if there is such a thing, is worse than no *satori*. See the following examples:

When Rinzai (Lin-chi) was meekly submitting to the thirty blows of Obaku (Huang-po), he presented a pitiable sight, but as soon as he had attained *satori* he was quite a different personage. His first exclamation was, "There is not much after all in the Buddhism of Obaku." And when he again saw the reproachful Obaku, he returned his favor by giving him a slap in the face. "What arrogance! What impudence!" one may think. But there was reason in Rinzai's rudeness; no wonder Obaku was quite pleased with this treatment.

When Tokusan (Te-shan) gained an insight into the truth of Zen he immediately took out all his commentaries on the *Diamond Sutra*, once so valued and considered indispensable that he had to carry them wherever he went, and set fire to them, reducing all the manuscripts to ashes. He exclaimed, "However deep one's knowledge of abstruse philosophy, it is like a piece of hair flying in the vastness of space; however important one's experience in things worldly, it is like a drop of water thrown into an unfathomable abyss."

One day, following the incident of the flying geese, to which reference was made elsewhere, Baso appeared in the preaching hall and was about to speak before a congregation, when Hyakujo, whose nose was literally put out of joint, came forward and began to roll up the matting which is spread before the Buddha for the master to kneel. The rolling up generally means the end of the sermon. Baso, without protesting, came down from the pulpit and returned to his room. He sent for Hyakujo and asked him why he rolled up the matting before he had even uttered a word. Replied Hyakujo, "Yesterday you twisted my nose and it was quite painful." Said Baso, "Where were your thoughts wandering?" Hyakujo replied, "Today it is no longer painful." With this Baso admitted Hyakujo's understanding.

These examples are sufficient to show what changes are produced in one's mind by the attainment of *satori*. Before *satori*, how helpless those monks were! They were like travelers lost in the desert. But after *satori* they behave like absolute monarchs; they are no longer slaves to anybody, they are themselves master.

—D. T. Suzuki

The Chess Game

A YOUNG MAN who had a bitter disappointment in life went to a remote monastery and said to the abbot: "I am disillusioned with life and wish to attain enlightenment to be freed from these sufferings. But I have no capacity for sticking long at anything. I could never do long years of meditation and study and austerity; I should relapse and be drawn back to the world again, painful though I know it to be. Is there any short way for people like me?" "There is," said the abbot, "if you are really determined. Tell me, what have you studied, what have you concentrated on most in your life?" "Why, nothing really. We were rich, and I did not have to work. I suppose the thing I was really interested in was chess. I spent most of my time at that."

The abbot thought for a moment, and then said to his attendant: "Call such-and-such a monk, and tell him to bring a chessboard and men." The monk came with the board and the abbot set up the men. He sent for a sword and showed it to the two. "O monk," he said, "you have vowed obedience to me as your abbot, and now I require it of you. You will play a game of chess with this youth, and if you lose I shall cut off your head with this sword. But I promise that you will be reborn in paradise. If you win, I shall cut off the head of this man;

chess is the only thing he has ever tried hard at, and if he loses he deserves to lose his head also." They looked at the abbot's face and saw that he meant it: he would cut off the head of the loser.

They began to play. With the opening moves the youth felt the sweat trickling down to his heels as he played for his life. The chessboard became the whole world; he was entirely concentrated on it. At first he had somewhat the worst of it, but then the other made an inferior move and he seized his chance to launch a strong attack. As his opponent's position crumbled, he looked covertly at him. He saw a face of intelligence and sincerity, worn with years of austerity and effort. He thought of his own worthless life, and a wave of compassion came over him. He deliberately made a blunder and then another blunder, ruining his position and leaving himself defenseless.

The abbot suddenly leaned forward and upset the board. The two contestants sat stupefied. "There is no winner and no loser," said the abbot slowly, "there is no head to fall here. Only two things are required," and he turned to the young man, "complete concentration, and compassion. You have today learned them both. You were completely concentrated on the game, but then in that concentration you could feel compassion and sacrifice your life for it. Now stay here a few months and pursue our training in this spirit and your enlightenment is sure." He did so and got it.

3

Salvation or Satori

ONE OF THE ERRORS which most surely hinder man's intemporal realization is that of seeing in this realization a compulsive character. In many "spiritual" systems, religious or otherwise, man has the "duty" of achieving his "salvation"; he denies all value to that which is temporal and concentrates all the reality imaginable on the "salvation." It is evident, however, that there is again here a form of idolatry, since realization, seen thus as something which excludes other things, is then only one thing among others, limited and formal, and that it is regarded at once as alone "sacred" and immeasurably superior to all the rest. All the determining, enslaving reality which man attributed to this or that "temporal" enterprise is crystallized now on the enterprise of "salvation," and this enterprise becomes the most determining, the most enslaving that can be imagined. Since realization signifies liberation one arrives at the absurd paradox that man is subjected to the coercive duty to be free. Man's distress is concentrated then on this question of his salvation; he trembles at the thought that he may die before having attained his deliverance. Such a grave error of understanding necessarily entails anxiety, inner agitation, a feeling of unworthiness, an egotistical crispation on oneself-as-a-distinct-being, that

47

is to say, it prevents inner pacification, reconciliation with oneself, disinterestedness toward oneself-as-a-distinct-being, the diminution of emotion—in short all the inner atmosphere of relaxation which governs the release of *satori*.

The man who deceives himself thus, however, can think again and better. There is no duty except in relation to an authority which imposes it. The believer of this or that religion will say that "God" is the authority which imposes on him the obligation of salvation. But who then is this "God" who while imposing something on me, is separate from me and has need of my action? Everything, then, is not included in his perfect harmony?

The same error is found among certain men sufficiently evolved intellectually no longer to believe in a personal God. They seem at least no longer to believe in him. If one looks more closely one perceives that they believe in him still. They imagine their *satori*, and themselves after their *satori*, and that is their personal God, a coercive idol, disquieting, implacable. They *must* realize themselves, they *must* liberate themselves, they are terrified at the thought of not being able to get there, and they are elated by any inner phenomenon which gives them hope. There is "spiritual ambition" in all this which is necessarily accompanied by the absurd idea of the Superman that they should become, with a demand for this becoming, and distress.

This error entails, in a fatally logical manner, the need to teach others. Our attitude toward others is modeled on our attitude toward ourselves. If I believe that I *must* achieve my "salvation" I cannot avoid believing that I *must* lead others to do the same. If the relative truth that I possess is associated in me with a duty to live this truth—duty depending on an idolatry, conscious or otherwise—the thought necessarily comes to me that it is my duty to communicate my truth to others. At the most this results in the Inquisition and the Dragonnades; at the least those innumerable sects, great and small, which throughout the whole of History have striven to influence the minds of men who never questioned them, of men who asked nothing of them.

The refutation of this error that we are here studying is perfectly expounded in Zen, and as far as we know, nowhere perfectly but there. Zen tells man that he is free now, that no chain exists which he needs to throw off; he has only the illusion of chains. Man will enjoy his freedom as soon as he ceases to believe that he needs to free himself, as soon as he throws from his shoulders the terrible duty of salvation. Zen demonstrates the nullity of all belief in a personal God, and the deplorable constraint that necessarily flows from this belief. It says: "Do not put any head above your own"; it says also: "Search not for the truth; only cease to cherish opinions."

Why then, some will say, should man strive to attain *satori*? To put such a question is to suppose absurdly that man cannot struggle toward *satori* except under the compulsion of a duty. *Satori* represents the end of this distress which is actually at the center of one's whole psychic life and in which one's joys are only truces; is it intelligent to ask me why I strive to obtain this complete and final relief? If anyone persists in asking I reply: "Because my life will be so much more agreeable afterward." And, if my understanding is right, I am not afraid that death may come, today or tomorrow, to interrupt my efforts before their attainment. Since the problem of my suffering ends with me why should I worry myself because I am unable to resolve it?

A clear understanding, on the other hand, neither forbids the teaching of others nor obliges one to undertake it; such a prohibition would represent an obligation as erroneous as the first. But the man who has understood that his own realization is not in any manner his duty contents himself with replying, if asked, that if he takes the initiative of speaking it will be only to propose such ideas with discretion, without experiencing any need of being understood. He is like a man who, possessing good food in excess, opens his door; if a passerby notices this food and comes in to eat it, well and good; if another does not come in, that is equally satisfactory. Our emotions, our desires, and our fears, have no place in a true understanding.

—Hubert Benoit

The Third Eye

LOOK WITHIN

Daiju visited the master Baso in China. Baso asked:
"What do you seek?"
"Enlightenment," replied Daiju.
"You have your own treasure house. Why do you search outside?" Baso asked.
Daiju inquired: "Where is my treasure house?"
Baso answered: "What you are asking is your treasure house."
Daiju was enlightened! Ever after he urged his friends: "Open your own treasure house and use those treasures."

᎒

His disciples said to him:
On what day will the rest of the dead take place?
And on what day does the new world come?
He said to them:
That rest for which you are waiting has come;
but you do not recognize it.

᎒

No paradise of the East,
No paradise of the West—
Seek along the way you have come.
They are all within you.

EMPTY YOUR CUP

Only when you have no thing in your mind and no mind in things are you vacant and spiritual, empty and marvelous.

૭

Jesus said:
    I stood in the midst of the world
    and I appeared to them in the flesh;
    I found all of them drunken;
    I found none among them thirsty.
    And my soul was pained for the children of men,
    for they are blind in their hearts,
    and they do not see
    that they came empty into the world
    seeking also to leave the world empty.
    But now they are drunken,
    When they throw off their wine,
    then they will repent.

૭

Nan-in, a Japanese master, received a university professor who came to inquire about Zen. Nan-in served tea. He poured his visitor's cup full, and then kept on pouring. The professor watched the overflow until he no longer could restrain himself. "It is over-full. No more will go in!" "Like this cup," Nan-in said, "you are full of your own opinions and speculations. How can I show you Zen unless you first empty your cup?"

THIS BEAUTIFUL MOON

If a man wants to sue you for your coat,
Let him have it and your overcoat as well.
If anybody forces you to go a mile with him,
Do more—go two miles with him.
Give to the man who asks anything from you,
And don't turn away from the man who wants to
      borrow.

❧

Ryokan, a Zen master, lived the simplest kind of life in a little hut at the foot of a mountain. One evening a thief visited the hut only to discover there was nothing in it to steal.

Ryokan returned and caught him. "You may have come a long way to visit me," he told the prowler, "and you should not return empty-handed. Please take my clothes as a gift."

The thief was bewildered. He took the clothes and slunk away.

Ryokan sat naked, watching the moon. "Poor fellow," he mused, "I wish I could give him this beautiful moon."

❧

The thief
   Left it behind—
      The moon at the window.

FINGER-CHOPPING ZEN

Jesus said:
> If your right eye leads you astray, tear it out and fling it away; it is better for you to lose one part of your body than for the whole of it to be thrown into hell. And if your right hand is your undoing, cut it off and fling it away; it is better for you to lose one part of your body than for the whole of it to go to hell.

ᐧ

Gutei raised his finger, whenever he was asked a question about Zen. A boy attendant began to imitate him in this way. When anyone asked the boy what his master had preached about, the boy would raise his finger.

Gutei heard about the boy's mischief. He seized him and cut off his finger. The boy cried and ran away. Gutei called and stopped him. When the boy turned his head to Gutei, Gutei raised up his own finger. In that instant the boy was enlightened.

Mumon's comment: Enlightenment, which Gutei and the boy attained, has nothing to do with a finger. If anyone clings to a finger, Gutei's teacher will be so disappointed that he will annihilate Gutei, the boy, and the clinger all together.

A RIDDLE

Jesus said:
Look upon the Living One as long as you live
    so that you will not die
    and seek to see him
    without being able to see him.

ᕯ

Like the empty sky it has no boundaries,
Yet it is right in this place, ever profound and clear.
When you seek to know it you cannot see it.
You cannot take hold of it,
But you cannot lose it.
In not being able to get it, you get it.
When you are silent, it speaks;
When you speak it is silent.
The great gate is wide open to bestow alms, and no
      crowd
Is blocking the way.

ᕯ

Jesus said:
I will give you
    what eye has not seen
    and ear has not heard
    and hand has not touched
    and which has not come into the heart of man.

WHAT IS IT?

SITTING QUIETLY

Sitting quietly, doing nothing,
Spring comes, and the grass grows by itself.

❧

Once upon a time there was a man standing on a high hill. Three travelers, passing in the distance, noticed him and began to argue about him. One said: "He has probably lost his favorite animal." Another said: "No, he is probably looking for his friend." The third said: "He is up there only in order to enjoy the fresh air." The three travelers could not agree and continued to argue right up to the moment when they arrived at the top of the hill. One of them asked: "O friend, standing on this hill, have you not lost your favorite animal?" "No, sir, I have not lost him." The other asked: "Have you not lost your friend?" "No, sir, I have not lost my friend either." The third traveler asked: "Are you not here in order to enjoy the fresh air?" "No, sir." "What then are you doing here, since you answer 'No' to all our questions?" The man on the hill replied: "I am just standing."

❧

When walking, just walk,
When sitting, just sit,
Above all, don't wobble.

TODODAY

How admirable,
He who thinks not, "Life is fleeting,"
When he sees the lightning!

᠗

Buddha told a parable in a sutra:

A man traveling across a field encountered a tiger. He fled, the tiger after him. Coming to a precipice, he caught hold of the root of a wild vine and swung himself down over the edge. The tiger sniffed at him from above. Trembling, the man looked down to where, far below, another tiger was waiting to eat him. Only the vine sustained him.

Two mice, one white and one black, little by little started to gnaw away the vine. The man saw a luscious strawberry near him. Grasping the vine with one hand, he plucked the strawberry with the other. How sweet it tasted!

᠗

Today while the blossoms
Still cling to the vine
I'll taste your strawberries
And drink your sweet wine.
A million tomorrows shall pass away
Ere I forget all the joys that are mine
Today.

PERFECT SILENCE

Bodhidharma, the first Zen patriarch, gathered his disciples about him to test their understanding. One said: "In my view, truth neither adheres to words nor is it separate from them." The Master said: "You have my flesh." Another spoke. "According to my belief, there is nothing to be grasped, reality is emptiness." To him the Master replied: "You have my bones." Finally there was Hui-ko: He bowed respectfully and stood silent. Bodhidharma said: "You have my marrow."

ဢ

> He who knows does not say;
> He who says does not know.
>
> —Lao Tzu

ဢ

Jesus said to his disciples:
　　Make comparisons; tell me what I am like.
Simon Peter said to him:
　　You are like a just angel.
Matthew said to him:
　　You are like a wise philosopher.
Thomas said to him:
　　Master, my mouth will in no way endure
　　my saying what you are like.
Jesus said:
　　I am not your master.

NOT FAR FROM BUDDHAHOOD

A university student while visiting Gasan asked him: "Have you ever read the Christian Bible?" "No, read it to me," said Gasan.

The student opened the Bible and read from St. Matthew: "And why take ye thought for raiment? Consider the lilies of the field, how they grow. They toil not, neither do they spin, and yet I say unto you that even Solomon in all his glory was not arrayed like one of these. . . . Take therefore no thought for the morrow, for the morrow shall take thought for the things of itself."

Gasan said: "Whoever uttered those words I consider an enlightened man."

The student continued reading: "Ask and it shall be given you, seek and ye shall find, knock and it shall be opened unto you. For everyone that asketh receiveth, and he that seeketh findeth, and to him that knocketh, it shall be opened."

Gasan remarked: "That is excellent. Whoever said that is not far from Buddhahood."

᠙

What then of the man who hears these words of mine and acts upon them? He is like a man who had the sense to build his house on rock. The rain came down, the floods rose, the wind blew, and beat upon that house; but it did not fall, because its foundations were on rock.

It

You WERE PROBABLY BROUGHT UP in a culture where the presiding image of IT has for centuries been God the Father, whose pronoun is He, because IT seems too impersonal and She would, of course, be inferior. Is this image still workable, as a functional myth to provide some consensus about life and its meaning for all the diverse peoples and cultures of this planet?

Frankly, the image of God the Father has become ridiculous—that is, unless you read St. Thomas Aquinas or Martin Buber or Paul Tillich, and realize that you can be a devout Jew or Christian without having to believe, literally, in the Cosmic Male Parent. Even then, it is difficult not to feel the force of the image, because images sway our emotions more deeply than conceptions. As a devout Christian you would be saying day after day the prayer "Our Father who art in heaven," and eventually it gets you: you are relating emotionally to IT as to an idealized father—male, loving but stern, and a personal being quite other than yourself. Obviously, you must be other than God so long as you conceive yourself as the separate ego, but when we realize that this form of identity is no more than a social institution, and one which has ceased to be a workable life-game, the sharp division between oneself and the ultimate reality is no longer relevant.

Furthermore, the younger members of our society have for some time been in growing rebellion against paternal authority and the paternal state. For one reason, the home in an industrial society is chiefly a dormitory, and the father does not work there, with the result that wife and children have no part in his vocation. He is just a character who brings in money, and after working hours he is supposed to forget about his job and have fun. Novels, magazines, television, and popular cartoons therefore portray "Dad" as an incompetent clown. And the image has some truth in it because Dad has fallen for the hoax that work is simply something you do to make money, and with money you can get anything you want.

It is no wonder that an increasing proportion of college students want no part in Dad's world, and will do anything to avoid the rat race of the salesman, commuter, clerk, and corporate executive. Professional men, too—architects, doctors, lawyers, ministers, and professors—have offices away from home, and thus, because the demands of their families boil down more and more to money, are ever more tempted to regard even professional vocations as ways of making money. All this is further aggravated by the fact that parents no longer educate their own children. Thus the child does not grow up with understanding of or enthusiasm for his father's work. Instead, he is sent to an understaffed school run mostly by women which, under the circumstances, can do no more than hand out mass-produced education which prepares the child for everything and nothing. It has no relation whatever to his father's vocation.

Along with this devaluation of the father, we are becoming accustomed to a conception of the universe so mysterious and so impressive that even the best father-image will no longer do for an explanation of what makes it run. But the problem then is that it is impossible for us to conceive an image higher than the human image. Few of us have ever met an angel, and probably would not recognize it if we saw one, and our images of an impersonal or suprapersonal God are hopelessly subhuman—jello, featureless light, homogenized space, or a whopping jolt of electricity. However, our image of man is changing as it becomes clearer and clearer that the human being is not simply and only his physical organism. My body is also my total environment, and this must be measured by light-years in the billions.

Hitherto the poets and philosophers of science have used the vast expanse and duration of the universe as a pretext for reflections on the unimportance of man, forgetting that man with "that enchanted loom, the brain" is precisely what transforms this immense electrical pulsation into light and color, shape and sound, large and small, hard and heavy, long and short. In knowing the world we humanize it, and if, as we discover it, we are astonished at its dimensions and its complexity, we should be just as astonished that we have the brains to perceive it.

Hitherto we have been taught, however, that we

are not really responsible for our brains. We do not know (in terms of words or figures) how they are constructed, and thus it seems that the brain and the organism as a whole are an ingenious vehicle which has been "given" to us, or an uncanny maze in which we are temporarily trapped. In other words, we accepted a definition of ourselves which confined the self to the source and to the limitations of conscious attention. This definition is miserably insufficient, for in fact we know how to grow brains and eyes, ears and fingers, hearts and bones, in just the same way that we know how to walk and breathe, talk and think—only we can't put it into words. Words are too slow and too clumsy for describing such things, and conscious attention is too narrow for keeping track of all their details.

Thus it will often happen that when you tell a girl how beautiful she is, she will say, "Now isn't that just like a man! All you men think about is bodies. OK, so I'm beautiful, but I got my body from my parents and it was just luck. I prefer to be admired for myself, not my chassis." Poor little chauffeur! All she is saying is that she has lost touch with her own astonishing wisdom and ingenuity, and wants to be admired for some trivial tricks that she can perform with her conscious attention. And we are all in the same situation, having dissociated ourselves from our bodies and from the whole network of forces in which bodies can come to birth and live.

Yet we can still awaken the sense that all this, too, is the self—a self, however, which is far beyond the image of the ego, or of the human body as limited by the skin. We then behold the Self where-ever we look, and its image is the universe in its light and in its darkness, in its bodies and in its spaces. This is the new image of man, but it is still an image. For there remains—to use dualistic words—"behind," "under," "encompassing," and "central" to it all the unthinkable IT, polarizing itself in the visible contrasts of waves and troughs, solids and spaces. But the odd thing is that this IT, however inconceivable, is no vapid abstraction: it is very simply and truly yourself.

In the words of a Chinese Zen master, "Nothing is left to you at this moment but to have a good laugh!" As James Broughton put it:

> This is It
> and I am It
> and You are It
> and so is That
> and He is It
> and She is It
> and It is It
> and That is That.

True humor is, indeed, laughter at one's Self—at the Divine Comedy, the fabulous deception, whereby one comes to imagine that a creature *in* existence is not also *of* existence, that what man is is not also what everything is. All the time we "know it in our bones" but conscious attention, distracted by details and differences, cannot see the whole for the parts. The major trick in this deception is, of course, death. Consider death as the permanent end of conscious-ness, the point at which you and your knowledge of the universe simply cease, and where you become as if you had never existed at all. Consider it also on a much vaster scale—the death of the universe at the time when all energy runs out, when, according to some cosmologists, the explosion which flung the galaxies into space fades out like a skyrocket. It will be as if it had never happened, which is, of course, the way things were before it *did* happen. Likewise, when you are dead, you will be as you were before you were conceived. So—there has been a flash, a flash of consciousness or a flash of galaxies. It happened. Even if there is no one left to remember.

But if, when it has happened and vanished, things are at all as they were before it began (including the possibility that there were no things), it can happen again. Why not? On the other hand, I might suppose that after it has happened things aren't the same as they were before. Energy was present before the explosion, but after the explosion died out, no energy was left. Forever and ever energy was latent. Then it blew up, and that was that. It is, perhaps, possible to imagine that what had always existed got tired of itself, blew up, and stopped. But this is a greater strain on my imagination than the idea that these flashes are periodic and rhythmic. They may go on and on, or round and round: it doesn't make much difference. Furthermore, if latent energy had *always* existed before the explosion, I find it difficult to think of a single, particular time coming when it had to stop. Can anything be half eternal? That is, can a process which had no beginning come to an end?

I presume, then, that with my own death I shall forget who I was, just as my conscious attention is unable to recall, if it ever knew, how to form the cells of the brain and the pattern of the veins. Conscious memory plays little part in our biological existence. Thus as my sensation of "I-ness," of being alive, once came into being without conscious memory or intent, so it will arise again and again, as the "central" Self—the IT—appears as the self/-other situation in its myriads of pulsating forms—always the same and always new, a here in the midst of a there, a now in the midst of then, and a one in the midst of many. And if I forget how many times I have been here, and in how many shapes, this forgetting is the necessary interval of darkness between every pulsation of light. I return in every baby born.

Actually, we know this already. After people die, babies are born—and, unless they are automata, every one of them is, just as *we* ourselves were, the "I" experience coming again into being. The conditions of heredity and environment change, but each of those babies incarnates the same experience of being central to a world that is "other." Each infant dawns into life as I did, without any memory of a past. Thus when I am gone there can be no experience, no living through, of the state of being a perpetual "has-been." Nature "abhors the vacuum" and the I-feeling appears again as it did before, and it matters not whether the interval be ten seconds or billions of years. In unconsciousness all times are the same brief instant.

This is so obvious, but our block against seeing

it is the ingrained and compelling myth that the "I" comes into this world, or is thrown out from it, in such a way as to have no essential connection with it. Thus we do not trust the universe to repeat what it has already done—to "I" itself again and again. We see it as an eternal arena in which the individual is no more than a temporary stranger— a visitor who hardly belongs—for the thin ray of consciousness does not shine upon its own source. In looking out upon the world, we forget that the world is looking at itself—through our eyes and IT's.

Now you know—even if it takes you some time to do a double take and get the full impact. It may not be easy to recover from the many generations through which the fathers have knocked down the children, like dominoes, saying, "Don't you dare think that thought! You're just a little upstart, just a creature, and you had better learn your place." On the contrary, you're IT. But perhaps the fathers were unwittingly trying to tell the children that IT plays IT cool. You don't come on (that is, on stage) like IT because you really are IT, and the point of the stage is to show on, not to show off. To come on like IT—to play at being God—is to play the Self as a role, which is just what it isn't. When IT plays, it plays at being everything else.

—Alan Watts

4

Riddles of Jesus

Jesus said:
  Blessed are the single ones and the elect,
    for you will find the kingdom.
  For you are from it,
    and you will enter into it again.

๏

Jesus said to them:
  When you make the two one,
  and make the inside like the outside,
  and the outside like the inside,
  and the upper side like the under side,
  and in such a way that you make the man
    with the woman a single one,
  in order that the man is not man and the
    woman is not woman; . . .
  then you will go into the kingdom.

๏

Jesus said:
  He who will drink from my mouth
    will become like me.
  I too will become he
    and the secrets will be revealed to him.

๏

Jesus said:
Perhaps men think that I came
to cast peace on the world;
and they do not know that I came
to cast divisions upon the earth,
fire, sword, war.
For five will be in a house;
there will be three against two and two against
three,
the father against the son and the son against the
father.
And they will stand because they are single ones.

❧

Jesus said:
The foxes have their holes and the birds have
their nest;
but the Son of Man has no place to lay his head
and to rest.

❧

Jesus said:
I am the light
which is over everything.
I am the All;
from me the All has gone forth,
and to me the All has returned.
Split wood: I am there.
Lift up the stone, and you will find me there.

❧

Jesus said:
    When you make the two one,
    you will become sons of man;
    and if you say, Mountain, be removed!
    it will move.

                    ⌒

The disciples said to Jesus:
    Tell us in what way our end will take place.
Jesus said:
    You have indeed uncovered the beginning
    so that you may seek the end;
    for in the place where the beginning is,
    there the end will be.
    Blessed is he who will stand in the beginning,
    and will know the end and will not taste death.

                    ⌒

Jesus said:
    Let him who seeks not cease in his seeking until
        he finds;
    and when he finds, he will be troubled,
    and if he is troubled, he will marvel,
    and will be a king over the All.

                    ⌒

Jesus said:
    The kingdom of the Father
    is like a merchant who had a cargo,
    and who found a pearl.
    He was a wise man.

He sold his cargo
and bought for himself the pearl alone.
You too seek for his treasure which does not
perish,
which abides where no moth enters to eat
and worms do not destroy.

෮

Jesus said:
If you do not fast to the world,
you will not find the kingdom;
if you do not truly keep the Sabbath,
you will not see the Father.

෮

And he said:
Man is like a wise fisherman, who cast his net
in the sea
and drew it out of the sea when it was full of
little fishes.
Among them the wise fisherman found a large
good fish.
He cast all the little fishes down into the sea.
He selected the large fish without difficulty.
He who has ears to hear, let him hear.

෮

Jesus said:
Many stand before the door,
but the single ones are those who will enter into
the bridechamber.

෮

The disciples said to Jesus:
   Tell us what the kingdom of heaven is like.
He said to them:
   It is like a grain of mustard, smaller than all the
      seeds.
   But when it falls on the earth which is tilled,
   it sends forth a great branch and becomes a
      covering
   for the birds of heaven.

᠃

Jesus said:
   Blessed is he who was before he became.
   If you are my disciples and hear my words,
   these stones will serve you.
   For you have five trees in paradise;
   they do not stir, summer or winter,
   and their leaves do not fall off.
   He who will understand them will not taste death.

᠃

Jesus said:
   He who has known the world has found a corpse,
   and he who has found a corpse,
   of him the world is not worthy.

᠃

His disciples said:
   Show us the place where you are,
   for it is necessary for us to seek it.

He said to them:
   He who has ears, let him hear!
   There is light within a light-man
   and it illuminates the whole world;
   if it does not illuminate it, it is darkness.

The Sound of One Hand

THE MASTER of Kennin temple was Mokurai, Silent Thunder. He had a little protégé named Toyo who was only twelve years old. Toyo saw the older disciples visit the master's room each morning and evening to receive instruction in *sanzen* or personal guidance in which they were given *koans* to stop mind-wandering.

Toyo wished to do *sanzen* also.

"Wait a while," said Mokurai. "You are too young."

But the child insisted, so the teacher finally consented.

In the evening little Toyo went at the proper time to the threshold of Mokurai's *sanzen* room. He struck the gong to announce his presence, bowed respectfully three times outside the door, and went to sit before the master in respectful silence.

"You can hear the sound of two hands when they clap together," said Mokurai. "Now show me the sound of one hand."

Toyo bowed and went to his room to consider this problem. From his window he could hear the music of the geishas. "Ah, I have it!" he proclaimed.

The next evening, when his teacher asked him to illustrate the sound of one hand, Toyo began to play the music of the geishas.

"No, no," said Mokurai. "That will never do. That is not the sound of one hand. You've not got it at all."

Thinking that such music might interrupt, Toyo moved his abode to a quiet place. He meditated again. "What can the sound of one hand be?" He happened to hear some water dripping. "I have it," imagined Toyo.

When he next appeared before his teacher, Toyo imitated dripping water.

"What is that?" asked Mokurai. "That is the sound of dripping water, but not the sound of one hand. Try again."

In vain Toyo meditated to hear the sound of one hand. He heard the sighing of the wind. But the sound was rejected.

He heard the cry of an owl. This also was refused.

The sound of one hand was not the locusts.

For more than ten times Toyo visited Mokurai with different sounds. All were wrong. For almost a year he pondered what the sound of one hand might be.

At last little Toyo entered true meditation and transcended all sounds. "I could collect no more," he explained later, "so I reached the soundless sound."

Toyo had realized the sound of one hand.

East and West

MANY ABLE THINKERS of the West, each from his specific point of view, have dealt with this time-worn topic, "East and West," but so far as I know there have been comparatively few Far Eastern writers who have expressed their views as Easterners. This fact has led me to choose this subject as a kind of preliminary to what will follow.

Basho (1644-94), a great Japanese poet of the seventeenth century, once composed a seventeen-syllable poem known as *haiku* or *hokku*. It runs, when translated into English, something like this:

> When I look carefully
> I see the *nazuna* blooming
> By the hedge!
>
> *Yoku mireba*
> *Nazuna hana saku*
> *Kakine kana.*

It is likely that Basho was walking along a country road when he noticed something rather neglected by the hedge. He then approached closer, took a good look at it, and found it was no less than a wild plant, rather insignificant and generally unnoticed by passersby. This is a plain fact described in the poem with no specifically poetic feeling expressed anywhere except perhaps in the last two syllables, which read in Japanese *kana*. This particle, frequently attached to a noun or an adjective or an adverb, signifies a certain feeling of admiration or praise or sorrow or joy, and can sometimes quite appropriately be rendered into English by an exclamation mark. In the present *haiku* the whole verse ends with this mark.

The feeling running through the seventeen, or rather fifteen, syllables with an exclamation mark at the end may not be communicable to those who are not acquainted with the Japanese language. I will try to explain it as best I can. The poet himself might not agree with my interpretation, but this does not matter very much if only we know that there is somebody at least who understands it in the way I do.

First of all, Basho was a nature poet, as most of the Oriental poets are. They love nature so much that they feel one with nature, they feel every pulse beating through the veins of nature. Most Westerners are apt to alienate themselves from nature. They think man and nature have nothing in common except in some desirable aspects, and that nature exists only to be utilized by man. But to Eastern people nature is very close. This feeling for nature was stirred when Basho discovered an inconspicuous, almost negligible plant blooming by the old dilapidated hedge along a remote country road, so innocently, so unpretentiously, not at all desiring to be noticed by anybody. Yet when one looks at it, how tender, how full of divine glory or splendor more glorious than Solomon's it is! Its very humbleness, its unostentatious beauty, evokes one's sincere admiration. The poet can read in every petal the deepest mystery of life or being. Basho might not have been conscious of it himself, but I am sure that in his heart at the time there were vibrations of feeling somewhat akin to what Christians may call divine love, which reaches the deepest depths of cosmic life.

The ranges of the Himalayas may stir in us the feeling of sublime awe; the waves of the Pacific may suggest something of infinity. But when one's mind is poetically or mystically or religiously opened, one feels as Basho did that even in every blade of grass there is something really transcending all venal, base human feelings, which lifts one to a realm equal in its splendor to that of the Pure Land. Magnitude in such cases has nothing to do with it. In this respect, the Japanese poet has a specific gift that detects something great in small things, transcending all quantitative measurements.

This is the East. Let me see now what the West has to offer in a similar situation. I select Tennyson. He may not be a typical Western poet to be singled out for comparison with the Far Eastern poet. But his short poem here quoted has something very closely related to Basho's. The verse is as follows:

> Flower in the crannied wall,
> I pluck you out of the crannies;—
> Hold you here, root and all, in my hand,
> Little flower—but if I could understand
> What you are, root and all, and all in all,
> I should know what God and man is.

There are two points I like to notice in these lines:

1. Tennyson's plucking the flower and holding it in his hand, "root and all," and looking at it, perhaps intently. It is very likely he had a feeling somewhat akin to that of Basho, who discovered a *nazuna* flower by the roadside hedge. But the difference between the two poets is: Basho does not pluck the flower. He just looks at it. He is absorbed in thought. He feels something in his mind, but he does not express it. He lets an exclamation mark say everything he wishes to say. For he has no words to utter; his feeling is too full, too deep, and has no desire to conceptualize it.

As to Tennyson, he is active and analytical. He first plucks the flower from the place where it grows. He separates it from the ground where it belongs. Quite differently from the Oriental poet, he does not leave the flower alone. He must tear it away from the crannied wall, "root and all," which means that the plant must die. He does not, apparently, care for its destiny; his curiosity must be satisfied. As some medical scientists do, he would vivisect the flower. Basho does not even touch the *nazuna*, he just looks at it, he "carefully" looks at it—that is all he does. He is altogether inactive, a good contrast to Tennyson's dynamism.

I would like to notice this point specifically here, and may have occasion to refer to it again. The East is silent, while the West is eloquent. But the silence of the East does not mean just to be dumb and remain wordless or speechless. Silence in many cases is as eloquent as being wordy. The West likes verbalism. Not only that, the West transforms the word into the flesh and makes this fleshiness come out sometimes too conspicuously, or rather too grossly and voluptuously, in its arts and religion.

2. What does Tennyson do next? Looking at the plucked flower, which is in all likelihood beginning to wither, he proposes the question within himself, "Do I understand you?" Basho is not inquisitive at all. He feels all the mystery as revealed in his humble *nazuna*—the mystery that goes deep into the source of all existence. He is intoxicated with this feeling and exclaims in an unutterable, inaudible cry.

Contrary to this, Tennyson goes on with his intellection: "*If* [which I italicize] I could understand you, I should know what God and man is." His appeal to the understanding is characteristically Western. Basho accepts, Tennyson resists. Tennyson's individuality stands away from the flower, from "God and man." He does not identify himself with either God or nature. He is always apart from them. His understanding is what people nowadays call "scientifically objective." Basho is thoroughly "subjective." (This is not a good word, for subject always is made to stand against object. My "subject" is what I like to call "absolute subjectivity.") Basho stands by this "absolute subjectivity" in which Basho sees the *nazuna* and the *nazuna* sees Basho. Here is no empathy, or sympathy, or identification for that matter.

Basho says: "look carefully" (in Japanese "*yoku mireba*"). The word "carefully" implies that Basho is no more an onlooker here but the flower has become conscious of itself and silently, eloquently expressive of itself. And this silent eloquence or eloquent silence on the part of the flower is humanly echoed in Basho's seventeen syllables. Whatever depth of feeling, whatever mystery of utterance, or even philosophy of "absolute subjectivity," there is, is intelligible only to those who have actually experienced all this.

In Tennyson, as far as I can see, there is in the first place no depth of feeling; he is all intellect, typical of Western mentality. He is an advocate of the Logos doctrine. He must say something, he must abstract or intellectualize on his concrete experience. He must come out of the domain of feeling into that of intellect and must subject living and feeling to a series of analyses to give satisfaction to the Western spirit of inquisitiveness.

I have selected these two poets, Basho and Tennyson, as indicative of two basic characteristic approaches to reality. Basho is of the East and Tennyson of the West. As we compare them we find that each bespeaks his traditional background. According to this, the Western mind is: analytical, discriminative, differential, inductive, individualistic, intellectual, objective, scientific, generalizing, conceptual, schematic, impersonal, legalisitc, organizing, power-wielding, self-assertive, disposed to impose its will upon others, etc. Against these Western traits those of the East can be characterized as follows: synthetic, totalizing, integrative, nondiscriminative, deductive, nonsystematic, dogmatic, intuitive (rather, affective), nondiscursive, subjective, spiritually individualistic and socially group-minded, etc. . . .

The Zen approach is to enter right into the object

itself and see it, as it were, from the inside. To know the flower is to become the flower, to be the flower, to bloom as the flower, and to enjoy the sunlight as well as the rainfall. When this is done, the flower speaks to me and I know all its secrets, all its joys, all its sufferings; that is, all its life vibrating within itself. Not only that: along with my "knowledge" of the flower I know all the secrets of the universe, which includes all the secrets of my own Self, which has been eluding my pursuit all my life so far, because I divided myself into a duality, the pursuer and the pursued, the object and the shadow. No wonder that I never succeeded in catching my Self, and how exhausting this game was!

Now, however, by knowing the flower I know my Self. That is, by losing myself in the flower I know my Self as well as the flower.

I call this kind of approach to reality the Zen way, the ante-scientific or metascientific or even antiscientific way.

This way of knowing or seeing reality may also be called conative or creative. While the scientific way kills, murders the object and by dissecting the corpse and putting the parts together again tries to reproduce the original living body, which is really a deed of impossibility, the Zen way takes life as it is lived instead of chopping it to pieces and trying to restore its life by intellection, or in abstraction gluing the broken pieces together. The Zen way preserves life as life; no surgical knife touches it. The Zen poet sings:

> All is left to her natural beauty,
> Her skin is intact,

85

Her bones are as they are:
There is no need for the paints, powders
of any tint.
She is as she is, no more, no less.
How marvelous!

The sciences deal with abstractions and there is no activity in them. Zen plunges itself into the source of creativity and drinks from it all the life there is in it. This source is Zen's Unconscious. The flower, however, is unconscious of itself. It is I who awaken it from the unconscious. Tennyson misses it when he plucks it from the crannied wall. Basho has it when he looks at the shyly blooming *nazuna* by the wild hedge. I cannot tell just where the unconscious is. Is it in me? Or is it in the flower? Perhaps when I ask, "Where?" it is nowhere. If so, let me be in it and say nothing.

—D. T. Suzuki

5

God and Meister Eckhart

THE STAGES OF ENLIGHTENMENT

Whoever understands the first truth
Should understand the ultimate truth.
The last and first,
Are they not the same?

In the first stage—the inner or new man, St. Augustine says, follows in the footsteps of good, pious people. He is still an infant at his mother's breast.

In the second stage—he no longer follows blindly the example even of good people. He goes in hot pursuit of sound instruction, godly counsel, holy wisdom. He turns his back on man and his face to God: leaving his mother's lap he smiles to his heavenly Father.

In the third stage—he parts more and more from his mother, draws farther and farther away from her breast. He flees care and casts away fear. Though he might with impunity treat everyone with harshness and injustice he would find no satisfaction in it, for in his love to God he is so much engaged with him, so much occupied with him in doing good: God has established him so firmly in joy, in holiness and love that everything unlike and foreign to God seems to him unworthy and repugnant.

In the fourth stage—he more and more grows and is rooted in love, in God. He is ever ready to welcome any struggle, any trial, adversity, or suffering, and that willingly, gladly, joyfully.

In the fifth stage—he is at peace, enjoying the fullness of supreme, ineffable wisdom.

In the sixth stage—he is de-formed and transformed by God's eternal nature. He has come to full perfection and, oblivious of impermanent things and temporal life, is drawn, transported, into the image of God and become a child of God. There is no further and no higher stage. It is eternal rest and bliss. The end of the inner and new man is eternal life.

> *Entering the forest he moves not the grass;*
> *Entering the water he makes not a ripple.*

FROM THE MEISTER

To get at the core of God at his greatest, one must first get into the core of himself at his least, for no one can know God who has not first known himself.

This core is a simple stillness, which is unmoved itself but by whose immobility all things are moved and all receive life, that is to say, all people who live by reason and have their center within themselves.

The eye by which I see God is the same as the

eye by which God sees me. My eye and God's eye are one and the same—one in seeing, one in knowing, and one in loving.

If it is true that God became man, it is also true that man became God . . . and so . . . you haven't got to borrow from God, for he is your own and therefore, whatever you get, you get from yourself.

For you will have peace to the extent that you have God, and the further you are away from God the less you will be at peace . . . Thus you may measure your progress with God by measuring your peace or the lack of it.

If you ask a good man: "Why are you seeking God?"—he will reply: "Just because he *is* God!" "Why are you seeking truth?" "Just because it *is* truth!" As life lives on for its own sake, needing no reason for being, so the just man has no reason for doing what he does.

The seed of God is in us. Given an intelligent and hard-working farmer, it will thrive and grow up to God, whose seed it is; and accordingly its fruits will be God-nature. Pear seeds grow into pear trees, nut seeds into nut trees, and God seed into God.

To the extent that you eliminate self from your activities, God comes into them—but not more and no less. Begin with that, and let it cost you your uttermost. In this way, and no other, is true peace to be found.

When I preach, I usually speak of disinterest and say that a man should be empty of self and all things.

We are to have what we have as if it were loaned to us and not given; to be without proprietary rights to body or soul, mind or faculties, worldly goods or honors, friends, relations, houses, castles, or anything else.

A man must become truly poor and as free from his own creaturely will as he was when he was born . . . He alone has true spiritual poverty who wills nothing, knows nothing, desires nothing.

Truly, I am so content with all God does, whether he gives or withholds, that there is not a cent's worth of difference between my condition and the best I could imagine for myself.

Who is Jesus? He has no name.

One bursts through creatures when he lets go of things he has loved.

A man has many skins in himself, covering the depths of his heart. Man knows so many things; he does not know himself. Why, thirty or forty skins or hides, just like an ox's or a bear's, so thick and hard, cover the soul. Go into your own ground and learn to know yourself there.

I tell you that no one can experience this birth (of God realized in the soul) without a mighty effort. No one can attain this birth unless he can withdraw his mind entirely from things.

As long as I am this or that, or have this or that, I am not all things and I have not all things. Become pure till you neither are nor have either this or that; then you are omnipresent and, being neither this nor that, are all things.

THE NAKED BOY

    Meister Eckhart met a beautiful naked boy.
      He asked him where he came from.
      He said: "I come from God."
      Where did you leave him?
      "In virtuous hearts."
      Where are you going?
      "To God."
      Where do you find him?
      "Where I part with all creatures."
      Who are you?
      "A king."
      Where is your kingdom?
      "In my heart."

Take care that no one divide it with you!
"I shall."
Then he led him to his cell.
Take whichever coat you will.
"Then I should be no king!"
And he disappeared.
For it was God himself—
Who was having a bit of fun.

Self-Knowledge

THE PROBLEMS OF THE WORLD are so colossal, so very complex, that to understand and so to resolve them one must approach them in a very simple and direct manner; and simplicity, directness, do not depend on outward circumstances nor on our particular prejudices and moods. As I was pointing out, the solution is not to be found through conferences, blueprints, or through the substitution of new leaders for old, and so on. The solution obviously lies in the creator of the problem, in the creator of the mischief, of the hate, and of the enormous misunderstanding that exists between human beings. The creator of this mischief, the creator of these problems, is the individual, you and I, not the world as we think of it. The world is your relationship with another. The world is not something separate from you and me; the world, society, is the relationship that we establish or seek to establish between each other.

So you and I are the problem, and not the world, because the world is the projection of ourselves and to understand the world we must understand ourselves. The world is not separate from us; we are the world, and our problems are the world's problems. This cannot be repeated too often, because we are so sluggish in our mentality that we think the world's problems are not our business, that they have to be resolved by the United Nations or by substituting new leaders for the old. It is a very dull mentality that thinks like that, because we are responsible for this frightful misery and confusion in the world, this ever-impending war. To transform the world, we must begin with ourselves; and what is important in beginning with ourselves is the intention. The intention must be to understand ourselves and not to leave it to others to transform themselves or to bring about a modified change through revolution, either of the left or of the right. It is important to understand that this is our responsibility, yours and mine; because, however small may be the world we live in, if we can transform ourselves, bring about a radically different point of view in our daily existence, then perhaps we shall affect the world at large, the extended relationship with others.

As I said, we are going to try and find out the process of understanding ourselves, which is not an isolating process. It is not withdrawal from the world, because you cannot live in isolation. To be is to be related, and there is no such thing as living in isolation. It is the lack of right relationship that brings about conflicts, misery, and strife; however small our world may be, if we can transform our relationship in that narrow world, it will be like a wave extending outward all the time. I think it is important to see that point, that the world is our relationship, however narrow; and if we can bring a transformation there, not a superficial but a radical transformation, then we shall begin actively to transform the world. Real revolution is not according to any particular pattern, either of the left or of the right, but it is a revolution of values, a revolution from sensate values to the values that are not sensate or created by environmental influences. To find these true values which will bring about a radical revolution, a transformation or a regeneration, it is essential to understand oneself. Self-knowledge is the beginning of wisdom, and therefore the beginning of transformation or regeneration. To understand oneself there must be the intention to understand—and that is where our difficulty comes in. Although most of us are discontented, we desire to bring about a sudden change, our discontent is canalized merely to achieve a certain result; being discontented, we either seek a different job or merely succumb to environment. Discontent, instead of setting us aflame, causing us to question life, the whole process of existence, is canalized, and thereby we become mediocre, losing that drive, that intensity to find out the whole significance of existence. Therefore it is important to discover these things for ourselves, because self-knowledge cannot be given to us by another, it is not to be found through any book. We must discover, and to discover there must be the intention, the search, the inquiry. So long as that intention to find out, to inquire deeply, is weak or does not exist, mere assertion or a casual wish to find out about oneself is of very little significance.

Thus the transformation of the world is brought about by the transformation of oneself, because the self is the product and a part of the total process of human existence. To transform oneself, self-knowledge is essential; without knowing what you are, there is no basis for right thought, and without knowing yourself there cannot be transformation. One must know oneself as one is, not as one wishes to be, which is merely an ideal and therefore fictitious, unreal; it is only that which *is* that can be transformed, not that which you wish to be. To know oneself as one is requires an extraordinary alertness of mind, because what *is* is constantly undergoing transformation, change, and to follow it swiftly the mind must not be tethered to any particular dogma or belief, to any particular pattern of action. If you would follow anything it is no good being tethered. To know yourself, there must be the awareness, the alertness of mind in which there is freedom from all beliefs, from all idealization because beliefs and ideals only give you a color, perverting true perception. If you want to know what you are you cannot imagine or have belief in something which you are not. If I am greedy, envious, violent, merely having an ideal of nonviolence, of nongreed, is of little value. But to know that one is greedy or violent, to know and understand it, requires an extraordinary perception, does it not? It demands honesty, clarity of thought, whereas to pursue an ideal away from what *is* is an escape; it prevents you from discovering and acting directly upon what you are.

The understanding of what you are, whatever it be—ugly or beautiful, wicked or mischievous—the understanding of what you are, without distortion, is the beginning of virtue. Virtue is essential, for it gives freedom. It is only in virtue that you can discover, that you can live—not in the *cultivation* of a virtue, which merely brings about respectability, not understanding and freedom. There is a difference between being virtuous and becoming virtuous. Being virtuous comes through the understanding of what *is*, whereas becoming virtuous is postponement, the covering up of what *is* with what you would like to be. Therefore in becoming virtuous you are avoiding action directly upon what *is*. This process of avoiding what *is* through the cultivation of the ideal is considered virtuous; but if you look at it closely and directly you will see that it is nothing of the kind. It is merely a postponement of coming face to face with what *is*. Virtue is not the becoming of what is not; virtue is the understanding of what *is* and therefore the freedom from what *is*. Virtue is essential in a society that is rapidly disintegrating. In order to create a new world, a new structure away from the old, there must be freedom to discover; and to be free, there must be virtue, for without virtue there is no freedom. Can the immoral man who is striving to becoming virtuous ever know virtue? The man who is not moral can never be free, and therefore he can never find out what reality is. Reality can be found only in understanding what *is*; and to understand what *is*, there must be freedom, freedom from the fear of what *is*.

To understand that process there must be the intention to know what *is*, to follow every thought, feeling and action; and to understand what *is* is extremely difficult, because what *is* is never still, never static, it is always in movement. The what *is* is what you are, not what you would like to be; it is not the ideal, because the ideal is fictitious, but it is actually what you are doing, thinking and feeling from moment to moment. What *is* is the actual, and to understand the actual requires awareness, a very alert, swift mind. But if we begin to condemn what *is*, if we begin to blame or resist it, then we shall not understand its movement. If I want to understand somebody, I cannot condemn him; I must observe, study him. I must love the very thing I am studying. If you want to understand a child, you must love and not condemn him. You must play with him, watch his movements, his idiosyncrasies, his ways of behavior; but if you merely condemn, resist or blame him, there is no comprehension of the child. Similarly, to understand what *is*, one must observe what one thinks, feels, and does from moment to moment. That is the actual. Any other action, any ideal or ideological action, is not the actual; it is merely a wish, a fictitious desire to be something other than what *is*.

To understand what *is* requires a state of mind in which there is no identification or condemnation, which means a mind that is alert and yet passive. We are in that state when we really desire to understand something; when the intensity of interest is there, that state of mind comes into being. When one is interested in understanding what *is*, the actual state of the mind, one does not need to force, discipline, or control it; on the contrary, there is passive alertness, watchfulness. This state of awareness comes when there is interest, the intention to understand.

The fundamental understanding of oneself does not come through knowledge or through the accumulation of experiences, which is merely the cultivation of memory. The understanding of oneself is from moment to moment; if we merely accumulate knowledge of the self, that very knowledge prevents further understanding, because accumulated knowledge and experience becomes the center through which thought focuses and has its being. The world is not different from us and our activities because it is what we are which creates the problems of the world; the difficulty with the majority of us is that we do not know ourselves directly, but seek a system, a method, a means of operation by which to solve the many human problems.

Now is there a means, a system, of knowing oneself? Any clever person, any philosopher, can invent a system, a method; but surely the following of a system will merely produce a result created by that system, will it not? If I follow a particular method of knowing myself, then I shall have the result which that system necessitates; but the result will obviously not be the understanding of myself. That is by following a method, a system, a means through which to know myself, I shape my thinking, my activities, according to a pattern; but the following of a pattern is not the understanding of oneself.

Therefore there is no method for self-knowledge. Seeking a method invariably implies the desire to attain some result—and that is what we all want. We follow authority—if not that of a person, then of a system, of an ideology—because we want a result which will be satisfactory, which will give us security. We really do not want to understand ourselves, our impulses and reactions, the whole process of our thinking, the conscious as well as the unconscious; we would rather pursue a system which assures us of a result. But the pursuit of a system is invariably the outcome of our desire for security, for certainty, and the result is obviously not the understanding of oneself. When we follow a method, we must have authorities—the teacher, the *guru*, the savior, the Master—who will guarantee us what we desire; and surely that is not the way to self-knowledge.

Authority prevents the understanding of oneself, does it not? Under the shelter of an authority, a guide, you may have temporarily a sense of security, a sense of well-being, but that is not the understanding of the total process of oneself. Authority in its very nature prevents the full awareness of oneself and therefore ultimately destroys freedom; in freedom alone can there be creativeness. There can be creativeness only through self-knowledge. Most of us are not creative; we are repetitive machines, mere gramophone records playing over and over again certain songs of experience, certain conclusions and memories, either our own or those of another. Such repetition is not creative being—but it is what we want. Because we want to be inwardly secure, we are constantly seeking methods and means for this security, and thereby we create authority, the worship of another, which destroys comprehension, that spontaneous tranquillity of mind in which alone there can be a state of creativeness.

Surely our difficulty is that most of us have lost this sense of creativeness. To be creative does not mean that we must paint pictures or write poems and become famous. That is not creativeness—it is merely the capacity to express an idea, which the public applauds or disregards. Capacity and creativeness should not be confused. Capacity is not creativeness. Creativeness is quite a different state of being, is it not? It is a state in which the self is absent, in which the mind is no longer a focus of our experiences, our ambitions, our pursuits, and our desires. Creativeness is not a continuous state, it is new from moment to moment, it is a movement in which there is not the "me," the "mine," in which the thought is not focused on any particular experience, ambition, achievement, purpose, and motive. It is only when the self is not that there is creativeness—that state of being in which alone there can be reality, the creator of all things. But that state cannot be conceived or imagined, it cannot be formulated or copied, it cannot be attained through any system, through any philosophy, through any discipline; on the contrary, it comes into being only through understanding the total process of oneself.

The understanding of oneself is not a result, a culmination; it is seeing oneself from moment to moment in the mirror of relationship—one's relationship to property, to things, to people, and to ideas. But we find it difficult to be alert, to be aware, and we prefer to dull our minds by following a method, by accepting authorities, superstitions, and gratifying theories; so our minds become weary, exhausted and insensitive. Such a mind cannot be in a state of creativeness. That state of creativeness comes only when the self, which is the process of recognition and accumulation, ceases to be; because, after all, consciousness as the "me" is the center of recognition, and recognition is merely the process of the accumulation of experience. But we are all afraid to be nothing, because we all want to be something. The little man wants to be a big man, the unvirtuous wants to be virtuous, the weak and obscure crave power, position, and authority. This is the incessant activity of the mind. Such a mind cannot be quiet and therefore can never understand the state of creativeness.

In order to transform the world about us, with its misery, wars, unemployment, starvation, class divisions, and utter confusion, there must be a transformation in ourselves. The revolution must begin within oneself—but not according to any belief or ideology, because revolution based on an idea, or in conformity to a particular pattern, is obviously no revolution at all. To bring about a fundamental revolution in oneself, one must understand the whole process of one's thought and feeling in relationship. That is the only solution to all our problems—not to have more disciplines, more beliefs, more ideologies, and more teachers. If we can understand ourselves as we are from moment to moment without the process of accumulation, then we shall see how there comes a tranquillity that is not a product of the mind, a tranquillity that is neither imagined nor cultivated; and only in that state of tranquillity can there be creativeness.

—J. Krishnamurti

Strong wine, fat meat, peppery things, very sweet things, these have not real taste; real taste is plain and simple. Supernatural, extraordinary feats do not characterize a real man; a real man is quite ordinary in behavior.

෨

Water not disturbed by waves settles down of itself. A mirror not covered with dust is clear and bright. The mind should be like this. When what beclouds it passes away, its brightness appears. Happiness must not be sought for; when what disturbs passes away, happiness comes of itself.

෨

At the sound of the bell in the silent night, I wake from my dream in this dream-world of ours. Gazing at the reflection of the moon in a clear pool, I see, beyond my form, my real form.

෨

The song of birds, the voices of insects, are all means of conveying truth to the mind; in flowers and grasses we see messages of the Way. The scholar, pure and clear of mind, serene and open of heart, should find in everything what nourishes him.

❦

Men know how to read printed books; they do not know how to read the unprinted ones. They can play on a stringed harp, but not on a stringless one. Applying themselves to the superficial instead of the profound, how should they understand music or poetry?

❦

If you know the inner significance of things, the misty moon of the Five Lakes is all within you. If you understand the activity of human phenomena, the heroism and nobility of the great men of all ages is in your grasp.

❦

Walking alone, leaning on a staff, in a valley of pine trees, clouds rise round my monkish robes. Sleeping with a book as my pillow by the window beneath the bamboos, I wake when the moonlight steeps the floor-cloths.

❦

A solitary cloud comes out of a mountain cave; it stays or departs without reference to anything else. The bright mirror of the moon hangs in the sky; it is aloof from both quietness and clamor.

❦

The Zen sect says, "When you are hungry, eat; when you are weary, sleep." Poetry aims at the description in common language of beautiful scenery. The sublime is contained in the ordinary, the hardest in the easiest. What is self-conscious and ulterior is far from the truth; what is mindless is near.

꩜

The body is like a boat adrift, floating along or motionless in a deep pool. The mind is like a piece of burnt wood; what matter if it is split fuel, or varnished with scented lacquer?

꩜

An ancient worthy says, "The shadow of the bamboo sweeps over the stairs, but the dust does not move. The disk of the moon passes through water of the lake, leaving no trace." One of our Confucians says, "The stream rushes down swiftly but all is silent around. The flowers fall incessantly, but we feel quiet." If you have grasped the meaning of this, in all your relations with things, you are free in mind and body.

꩜

If your heart is without stormy waves, everywhere are blue mountains and green trees. If our real nature is creative like nature itself, wherever we may be, we see that all things are free like sporting fishes and circling kites.

꩜

When in the mood, I take off my shoes and walk barefooted through the sweet-smelling grasses of the fields, wild birds without fear accompanying me. My heart at one with nature, I loosen my shirt as I sit absorbed beneath the falling petals, while the clouds silently enfold me as if wishing to keep me there.

෬

Just as a whirlwind roaring down a valley leaves nothing behind it, so the ear is to have nothing to do with right and wrong. Just as the moon only reflects its light in a pool, so the mind, empty and unattached, does not know itself and the outside world as two things.

6

This Is My Body

THERE HAS NOT YET existed a religion or a philosophy in which there is a true marriage of Heaven and Earth. There have been many approximations, but never one in which each said to the other, without any shadow of reservation, "I love you with all my heart!" We have seen the spiritual reduced to the material, and the material vaporized in the spiritual. We have seen unhappy compromises in which the spiritual is always saying to the material, "Yes, but . . ." We have seen the material perpetually damned with faint praise and always being talked down for the odd reason that it constantly changes and flows away, as if that were something wrong. Only most occasionally have Hindus had the courage to swing fully with the Lord in dancing his *maya,* and to stop insinuating that in some nasty, niggling last analysis the physical universe shouldn't be happening. Christian theologians, too, seem to have a commission to *protect* the Deity from full union with his universe, as if this would somehow completely subvert his morals. Indeed, they allow that the creature may participate in, reflect, be adopted into, transfigured by, or given unity with his Creator. But always, at the end of the line, there is someone wagging his finger and saying, "But . . .

never forget, little creature, that you are nothing, nothing right down to your miserable essence, for your being is not your own." So—my body is God's, my mind is God's, my being itself is God's, all on loan to nothing and no one.

But if I'm not here, I know Who is!

The basic difficulty seems to be that people in religious circles always need someone or something to blame. I even catch myself doing it when I think about Baptist preachers. Religion somehow attracts those who like to lay down the law and point the finger of accusation, seldom realizing, incidentally, that the congregation just adores a colorful scolding. So I would like to say this without condemning anyone, preachers included. The thing is to see all faces as the masks of God, all characters as his roles, preachers included. Toward the end of his life that extraordinary Hindu-Buddhist-Muslim saint, the poet Kabir, used to look around and ask, "To whom shall I preach?" He saw the face and the activity of his Beloved in every direction.

Obviously, as so many Christians seem to fear, this vision of God-as-all might be used as a rationalization for indulgence in total wickedness. But fire is not untrue, or something to be abolished, because it can be used to burn people alive. What they really seem to fear is that, if God is all in all, the wicked will not get their just deserts; someone may lose the satisfaction of knowing that evildoers are going to be boiled in oil and devoured by spiders forever and ever. At this point it becomes more and more difficult to separate the wicked from the moralists who want to see them properly judged.

In a larger perspective these theological objections are trivial. They are like avoiding broiled salmon for fear of the bones, or living for fear of dying. It is all a colossal haggling and footling over technicalities, a metaphysical filibuster subconsciously designed to postpone the great moment of awakening. Perhaps it is like a woman being interminably difficult to woo, so as to build up all that more passion for the moment when she finally yields. Enough, however, is enough. The moment has arrived when a really thoroughgoing spiritual materialism is the intelligent and essential attitude for the management of technology, and for helping mankind to be something better than the most predatory monster yet evolved.

In fact, it is impossible to be a true materialist without being a mystic as well. The would-be materialist who renounces mysticism is either a slob or a bore. Or both, for there is something profoundly dreary about mere sensuality—the unrelieved panorama of filet mignon, bosoms and bottoms, Chateauneuf-du-Pape, Alfa Romeos and Chris-Crafts, dry martinis, scrolls by Sesshu, Pro Musica on hi-fi, Chanel No. 5, and even alas, water, clouds, light, sand, and mountains beyond. After a while the bottoms feel like plastic. Still more dreary is the *sensible* materialism of the practical and provident, who will scrounge all their lives to provide themselves with leisure when they can no longer enjoy it. Or the academic materialist who is, perhaps, a scientific empiricist or a logical positivist or a "sound" statistical psychologist, whose real aim is to demonstrate that all nature is perfectly banal and dull.

The trouble with this fellow is that no one ever mixed raven's blood with his mother's milk. He is marvelously and uncannily bereft of any sense that existence is odd.

At the other extreme, the pure mystic is like pure alcohol, or like a wine without body. Intense, strongly principled, quiet-mannered and unobtrusive, devastatingly simple in his needs and colorless in his tastes—no belly-laugh, no good roll with a girl in the hay, no gentle grin of understanding as between man and man—this one, with his terrifying sincerity, is more of a Euclidean proposition than a human being. Spirituality needs a beer and a loud burp, just as sensuality needs a bed on the hard ground, a rough blanket, and a long look at the utterly improbable stars.

The difficulty with the material world is that it collapses when you lean on it and turns to a fine powder when you clutch it. Material pleasure, even of the most refined order, is never enough, if "enough" is what you are seeking. If there is that strange, deep longing in the heart for something that is "the answer"—the gorgeous, golden glory you have always wanted but have never been able to find or define, the thing that is finally for real and for keeps, the eternal home—then anything in the physical or intellectual universe that is asked to be *that* will collapse. But it is sour grapes to despise the material world for that reason.

The answer, the eternal home, will never, never be found so long as you are seeking it, for the simple reason that it is yourself—not the self that you are aware of and that you can love or hate, but the one that always vanishes when you look for it. As soon as you realize that you *are* the Center, you have no further need to see it, to try to make it an object or an experience. This is why the mystics call the highest knowledge unknowing.

—Alan Watts

Tail Waggers

WAG YOUR TAIL

Chuang Tzu was fishing in the P'u when the Prince of Ch'u sent two high officials to ask him to take charge of the administration of the Ch'u State.

Chuang Tzu went on fishing and, without turning his head, said: "I have heard that in Ch'u there is a sacred tortoise which has been dead now some three thousand years, and that the Prince keeps this tortoise carefully enclosed in a chest on the altar of his ancestral temple. Now, would this tortoise rather be dead and have its remains venerated, or be alive and wagging its tail in the mud?"

"It would rather be alive," replied the two officials, "and wagging its tail in the mud."

"Begone!" cried Chuang Tzu. "I too will wag my tail in the mud."

HORSING AROUND

There was a man who dearly loved his horse. He carried away its droppings in a basket; he scooped up its stale in a clamshell. One day a fly attached itself to the animal, and this man scotched it. Taken by surprise the horse began to plunge and rear, broke its halter, bruised its head, tore its breast. His intentions were for the creature's good; but it was his affection for it that proved the cause of its undoing.

BUTTERFLY

Once upon a time, I, Chuang Tzu, dreamt I was a butterfly, fluttering hither and thither, to all intents and purposes a butterfly. I was conscious only of following my fancies as a butterfly, and was unconscious of my individuality as a man. Suddenly, I awoke, and there I lay, myself again. Now I do not know whether I was then a man dreaming I was a butterfly, or whether I am now a butterfly dreaming I am a man.

THE ART OF ARCHERY

Lieh-tzu exhibited his skill in archery to Po-hun Wu-jen. When the bow was drawn to its full length, a cup of water was placed on his elbow, and he began to shoot. As soon as the first arrow was let fly, a second one was already on the string, and a third followed. In the meantime, he stood unmoved like a statue. Po-hun Wu-jen said, "The technique of shooting is fine, but it is not shooting of nonshooting. Let us go up to a high mountain and stand on a projecting rock over the precipice ten thousand feet high, and you try to shoot."

They now climbed up a high mountain; standing on a projecting rock over a precipice ten thousand feet high, Po-hun Wu-jen stepped backward with one-third of his feet hanging off the rock. He then motioned to Lieh-tzu to come forward. Lieh-tzu fell on the ground with perspiration flowing down to the heels.

Said Po-hun Wu-jen: "The perfect man soars up above the blue sky or dives down to the yellow springs, or wanders about all over the eight limits of the world, yet shows no signs of change in his spirit. But you betray a sign of trepidation and your eyes are dazed. How can you expect to hit the target?"

THE DRUNK

A drunken man who falls out of a cart, though he may suffer, does not die. His bones are the same as other people's; but he meets his accident in a different way. His spirit is in a condition of security. He is not conscious of riding in the cart; neither is he conscious of falling out of it. Ideas of life, death, fear, etc., cannot penetrate his breast; and so he does not suffer from contact with objective existences. And if such security is to be got from wine, how much more is it to be got from God. It is in God that the sage seeks his refuge and so he is free from harm.

PLEASURE OF FISHES

Chuang Tzu and Hui Tzu had strolled onto the bridge over the Hao, when the former observed: "See how the minnows are darting about! That is the pleasure of fishes."

"Not being a fish yourself," said Hui Tzu, "how can you possibly know in what consists the pleasure of fishes?"

"And not being I," retorted Chuang Tzu, "how can you know that I do not know?"

"If I, not being you, cannot know what you know," urged Hui Tzu, "it follows that you, not being a fish, cannot know in what consists the pleasure of fishes."

"Let us go back," said Chuang Tzu, "to your original question. You asked me how I knew in what consists the pleasure of fishes. Your very question shows that you knew I knew. I knew it from my own feelings on this bridge."

THE EMPTY BOAT

Suppose a boat is crossing a river and another boat, an empty one, is about to collide with it. Even an irritable man would not lose his temper. But suppose there was someone in the second boat. Then the occupant of the first would shout to him to keep clear. And if he did not hear the first time, nor even when called to three times, bad language would inevitably follow. In the first case there was no anger, in the second there was—because in the first case the boat was empty, in the second it was occupied. And so it is with man. If he could only pass empty through life, who would be able to injure him?

THE HUNCHBACK

There was a hunchback named Su. His jaws touched his navel. His shoulders were higher than his head. His hair knot looked up to the sky. His viscera were upside down. His buttocks were where his ribs should have been. By tailoring, or washing, he was easily able to earn his living. By sifting rice he could make enough to support a family of ten. When orders came down for a conscription, the hunchback stood unconcerned among the crowd. And, similarly, in matters of public works, his deformity shielded him from being employed.

On the other hand, when it came to donations of grain, the hunchback received as much as three *chung*, and of firewood ten faggots. And if physical deformity was thus enough to preserve his body until its allotted end, how much more would not moral and mental deformity avail!

WHY MOURN?

When Chuang Tzu's wife died, Hui Tzu went to condole. He found the widower sitting on the ground, singing, with his legs spread out at a right angle, and beating time on a bowl.

"To live with your wife," exclaimed Hui Tzu,

"and see your eldest son grow up to be a man, and then not to shed a tear over her corpse—this would be bad enough. But to drum on a bowl, and sing; surely this is going too far."

"Not at all," replied Chuang Tzu. "When she died, I could not help being affected by her death. Soon, however, I remembered that she had already existed in a previous state before birth, without form, or even substance; that while in that unconditioned condition, substance was added to spirit; that this substance then assumed form; and that the next stage was birth. And now, by virtue of a further change, she is dead, passing from one phase to another like the sequence of spring, summer, autumn, and winter. And while she is thus lying asleep in eternity, for me to go about weeping and wailing would be to proclaim myself ignorant of these natural laws. Therefore I refrain."

.

THREE IN THE MORNING

What is meant by "Three in the Morning"? In Sung there was a keeper of monkeys. Bad times came and he was obliged to tell them that he must reduce their ration of nuts. "It will be three in the morning and four in the evening," he said. The monkeys were furious. "Very well then," he said, "you shall have four in the morning and three in the evening." The monkeys accepted with delight.

THE USELESS TREE

Tzu Ch'i of Nan-poh was traveling on the Shang mountain when he saw a large tree which astonished him very much. A thousand chariot teams could have found shelter under its shade.

"What tree is this?" cried Tzu Ch'i. "Surely it must have unusually fine timber." Then, looking up, he saw that its branches were too crooked for rafters, while the trunk's irregular grain made it valueless for coffins. He tasted a leaf, but it took the skin off his lips, and its odor was so strong that it would make a man drunk for three days together.

"Ah!" said Tzu Ch'i. "This tree is good for nothing, and that is how it attained this size. A wise man might well follow its example."

WHERE IS TAO?

Tung Kuo Tzu asked Chuang Tzu, saying, "What you call Tao—where is it?"

"There is nowhere," replied Chuang Tzu, "where it is not."

"Tell me one place at any rate where it is," said Tung Kuo Tzu.

"It is in the ant," replied Chuang Tzu.

"Why get so low down?" asked Tung Kuo Tzu.

"It is in a tare," said Chuang Tzu.

"Still lower," objected Tung Kuo Tzu.

"It is in a potsherd," said Chuang Tzu.

"Worse still!" cried Tung Kuo Tzu.

"It is in ordure," said Chuang Tzu. And Tung Kuo Tzu made no reply.

CHUANG TZU'S DEATH

When Chuang Tzu was about to die, his disciples expressed a wish to give him a splendid funeral. But Chuang Tzu said, "With heaven and earth for my coffin and shell; with the sun, moon, and stars as my burial regalia; and with all creation to escort me to the grave, are not my funeral paraphernalia ready to hand?"

"We fear," argued the disciples, "lest the carrion kite should eat the body of our Master"; to which Chuang Tzu replied, "Above ground I shall be food for kites; below I shall be food for mole-crickets and ants. Why rob one to feed the other?"

FLOWING WITH LIFE

Confucius was looking at the cataract at Luliang. It fell from a height of two hundred feet, and its foam reached fifteen miles away. No scaly, finny creature could enter therein. Yet Confucius saw an old man go in, and thinking that he was suffering from some trouble and desirous of ending his life, bade a disciple run along the side to try and save him. The old man emerged about a hundred paces off, and flowing hair went caroling along the bank. Confucius followed him and said, "I had thought, sir, you were a spirit, but now I see you are a man. Kindly tell me, is there any way to deal thus with water?"

"No," replied the old man, "I have no way . . . plunging in with the whirl, I come out with the swirl. I accommodate myself to the water, not the water to me. And so I am able to deal with it after this fashion."

Credo

I believe that man is the product of natural evolution; that he is part of nature and yet transcends it, being endowed with reason and self-awareness.

I believe that man's essence is ascertainable. However, this essence is not a substance which characterizes man at all times through history. The essence of man consists in the above-mentioned contradiction inherent in his existence, and this contradiction forces him to react in order to find a solution. Man cannot remain neutral and passive toward this existential dichotomy. By the very fact of his being human, he is asked a question by life; how to overcome the split between himself and the world outside of him in order to arrive at the experience of unity and oneness with his fellow man and with nature. Man has to answer this question every moment of his life. Not only—or even primarily—with thoughts and words, but by his mode of being and acting.

I believe that there are a number of limited and ascertainable answers to this question of existence (the history of religion and philosophy is a catalogue of these answers); yet there are basically only two categories of answers. In one, man attempts to find again harmony with nature by regression to a pre-human form of existence, eliminating his specifically human qualities of reason and love. In the other, his goal is the full development of his human powers until he reaches a new harmony with his fellow man and with nature.

I believe that the first answer is bound to failure. It leads to death, destruction, suffering, and never to the full growth of man, never to harmony and strength. The second answer requires the elimination of greed and egocentricity, it demands discipline, will, and respect for those who can show the way. Yet, although this answer is the more difficult one, it is the only answer which is not doomed to failure. In fact, even before the final goal is reached, the activity and effort expended in approaching it has a unifying and integrating effect which intensifies man's vital energies.

I believe that man's basic alternative is the choice between life and death. Every act implies this choice. Man is free to make it, but this freedom is a limited one. There are many favorable and unfavorable conditions which incline him—his psychological constitution, the condition of the specific society into which he was born, his family, teachers, and the friends he meets and chooses. It is man's task to enlarge the margin of freedom, to strengthen the conditions which are conducive to life as against those which are conducive to death. Life and death, as spoken of here, are not the biological states, but states of being, of relating to the world. Life means constant change, constant birth. Death means cessation of growth, ossification, repetition. The unhappy fate of many is that they do not make the choice. They are neither alive nor dead. Life becomes a burden, an aimless enterprise, and busyness is the means to protect one from the torture of being in the land of shadows.

I believe that neither life nor history has an ultimate meaning which in turn imparts meaning to the life of the individual or justifies his suffering. Considering the contradictions and weaknesses which beset man's existence it is only too natural that he seeks for an "absolute" which gives him the illusion of certainty and relieves him from conflict, doubt, and responsibility. Yet, no god, neither in theological, philosophical, or historical garments, saves or condemns man. Only man can find a goal for life and the means for the realization of this goal. He cannot find a saving ultimate or absolute answer but he can strive for a degree of intensity, depth, and clarity of experience which gives him the strength to live without illusions, and to be free.

I believe that no one can "save" his fellow man by making the choice for him. All that one man can do for another is to show him the alternatives truthfully and lovingly, yet without sentimentality or illusion. Confrontation with the true alternatives may awaken all the hidden energies in a person, and enable him to choose life as against death. If he cannot choose life, no one else can breathe life into him.

I believe that there are two ways of arriving at the choice of the good. The first is that of duty and obedience to moral commands. This way can be effective, yet one must consider that in thousands of years only a minority have fulfilled even the requirements of the Ten Commandments. Many more have committed crimes when they were presented to them as commands by those in authority. The other way is to develop a taste for and a sense of well-being in doing what is good or right. By taste for well-being, I do not mean pleasure in the Benthamian or Freudian sense. I refer to the sense of heightened aliveness in which I confirm my powers and my identity.

I believe that education means to acquaint the young with the best heritage of the human race. But while much of this heritage is expressed in words, it is effective only if these words become reality in the person of the teacher and in the practice and structure of society. Only the idea which has materialized in the flesh can influence man; the idea which remains a word only changes words.

I believe in the perfectibility of man. This perfectibility means that man *can* reach his goal, but it does not mean that he *must* reach it. If the individual will not choose life and does not grow, he will by necessity become destructive, a living corpse. Evilness and self-loss are as real as are goodness and aliveness. They are the secondary potentialities of man if he chooses not to realize his primary potentialities.

I believe that only exceptionally is a man born as a saint or as a criminal. Most of us have dispositions for good and for evil, although the respective weight of these dispositions varies with individuals. Hence, our fate is largely determined by those influences which mold and form the given dispositions. The family is the most important influence. But the family itself is mainly an agent of society, the transmission belt for those values and norms which a society wants to impress on its members. Hence, the most important factor for the development of the individual is the structure and the values of the society into which he has been born.

I believe that society has both a furthering and an inhibiting function. Only in cooperation with others, and in the process of work, does man develop his powers, only in the historical process does he create himself. But at the same time, most societies until now have served the aims of the few who wanted to use the many. Hence they had to use their power to stultify and intimidate the many (and thus, indirectly, themselves), to prevent them from developing all their powers; for this reason society has always conflicted with humanity, with the universal norms valid for every man. Only when society's aim will have become identical with the aims of humanity, will society cease to cripple man and to further evil.

I believe that every man represents humanity. We are different as to intelligence, health, talents. Yet we are all one. We are all saints and sinners, adults and children, and no one is anybody's superior or judge. We have all been awakened with the Buddha, we have all been crucified with Christ, and we have all killed and robbed with Genghis Khan, Stalin, and Hitler.

I believe that man can visualize the experience of the whole universal man only by realizing his individuality and never by trying to reduce himself to an abstract, common denominator. Man's task in life is precisely the paradoxical one of realizing his individuality and at the same time transcending it and arriving at the experience of universality. Only the fully developed individual self can drop the ego.

I believe that the One World which is emerging can come into existence only if a New Man comes into being—a man who has emerged from the archaic ties of blood and soil, and who feels himself to be the son of man, a citizen of the world whose loyalty is to the human race and to life, rather than to any exclusive part of it; a man who loves his country because he loves mankind, and whose judgment is not warped by tribal loyalties.

I believe that man's growth is a process of continuous birth, of continuous awakening. We are usually half asleep and only sufficiently awake to go about our business; but we are not awake enough to go about living, which is the only task that matters for a living being. The great leaders of the human race are those who have awakened man from his half-slumber. The great enemies of humanity are those who put it to sleep, and it does not matter whether their sleeping potion is the worship of God or that of the Golden Calf.

I believe that the development of man in the last four thousand years of history is truly awe-inspiring. He has developed his reason to a point where he is solving the riddles of nature, and has emancipated himself from the blind power of the natural forces. But at the very moment of his greatest triumph, when he is at the threshold of a new world, he has succumbed to the power of the very things and organizations he has created. He has invented a new method of producing, and has made production and distribution his new idol. He worships the work of his hands and has reduced himself to being the servant of things. He uses the name of God, of freedom, of humanity, of socialism, in vain; he prides himself on his powers—the bombs and the machines—to cover up his human bankruptcy; he boasts of his power to destroy in order to hide his human impotence.

I believe that the only force that can save us from self-destruction is reason; the capacity to recognize the unreality of most of the ideas that man holds, and to penetrate to the reality veiled by the layers and layers of deception and ideologies; reason, not as a body of knowledge, but as a "kind of energy, a force which is fully comprehensible only in its agency and effects . . ." a force whose "most important function consists in its power to bind and to dissolve."* Violence and arms will not save us; sanity and reason may.

I believe that reason cannot be effective unless man has hope and belief. Goethe was right when he said that the deepest distinction between various historical periods is that between belief and disbelief, and when he added that all epochs in which belief dominates are brilliant, uplifting, and fruitful, while those in which disbelief dominates vanish because nobody cares to devote himself to the unfruitful. No doubt the thirteenth century, the Renaissance, the Enlightenment, were ages of belief and hope. I am afraid that the Western World in the twentieth century deceives itself about the fact that it has lost hope and belief. Truly, where there

* Ernst Cassirer, *The Philosophy of the Enlightenment* (Boston: Beacon Press, 1955), p. 13.

131

is no belief in man, the belief in machines will not save us from vanishing; on the contrary, this "belief" will only accelerate the end. Either the Western World will be capable of creating a renaissance of humanism in which the fullest developments of man's humanity, and not production and work, are the central issues—or the West will perish as many other great civilizations have.

I believe that to recognize the truth is not primarily a matter of intelligence, but a matter of character. The most important element is the courage to say *no*, to disobey the commands of power and of public opinion; to cease being asleep and to become human; to wake up and lose the sense of helplessness and futility. Eve and Prometheus are the two great rebels whose very "crimes" liberated mankind. But the capacity to say "no" meaningfully implies the capacity to say "yes" meaningfully. The "yes" to God is the "no" to Caesar; the "yes" to man is the "no" to all those who want to enslave, exploit, and stultify him.

I believe in freedom, in man's right to be himself, to assert himself and to fight all those who try to prevent him from being himself. But freedom is more than the absence of violent oppression. It is more than "freedom from." It is "freedom to"—the freedom to become independent; the freedom to *be* much, rather than to *have* much, or to *use* things and people. . . .

I believe that man must get rid of illusions that enslave and paralyze him; that he must become aware of the reality inside and outside of him in

order to create a world which needs no illusions.
Freedom and independence can be achieved only
when the chains of illusion are broken.

—Erich Fromm

Other MENTOR Titles of Related Interest